Medicare Handbook
For Beginners

A Complete Guide to the Plans, Benefits, and Informed
Choice Making for Better Health Coverage

Alden Royce

TABLE OF CONTENTS

CHAPTER 1

INTRODUCTION TO MEDICARE

Overview of Medicare

Medicare, established in 1965, is a federal health insurance program designed for individuals aged 65 and above, without considering their income, medical history, or health condition. In 1972, the program expanded to include individuals under 65 with long-term disabilities. Currently, Medicare plays a crucial role in ensuring that around 60 million older adults and younger individuals with disabilities have access to affordable healthcare and financial support. In 2017, the program helps pay for a lot of different kinds of medical care, like stays in hospitals, visits to the doctor, prescription drugs, preventative care, skilled nursing facility and home health care, hospice care, and more. Five percent of all government spending and twenty percent of all national health spending went to Medicare. The majority of individuals aged 65 or older are eligible for Medicare Part A if they or their spouse qualify for Social Security. Those who have paid payroll taxes for at least 10 years are exempt from paying a premium for Part A. For individuals under 65 receiving Social Security Disability Insurance (SSDI), there is generally a two-year waiting period before they can enroll in Medicare. However, those diagnosed with end-stage renal disease (ESRD) or amyotrophic lateral sclerosis (ALS) are eligible to join Medicare immediately.

Characteristics of People on Medicare

A lot of Medicare recipients have health problems, like multiple chronic conditions that make it hard for them to do daily tasks, and a lot of them live on low budgets. There were 32% of people in 2016 who couldn't do certain things, 25% who said they were in good or poor health, and 22% who had five or more chronic diseases (Figure 1). One in seven beneficiaries (15%) was younger than 65 and had a long-term disability. One in two beneficiaries (1.2%) was 85 or older. In 2013, a little over two million beneficiaries (3%) lived in a long-term care home. Half of the people on Medicare in 2016 had incomes less than $26,200 per person and savings below $74,450.

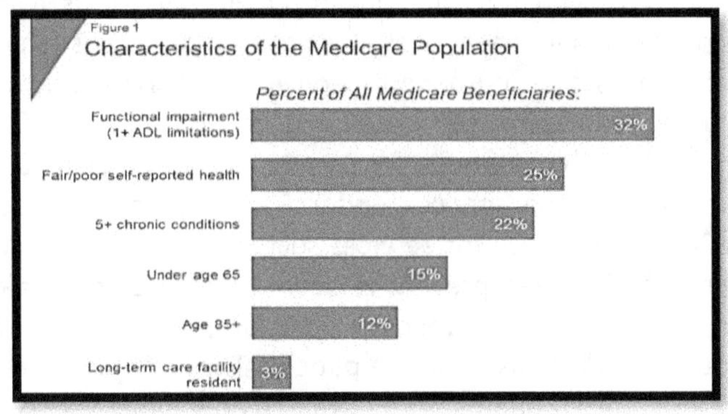

Figure 1: Characteristics of the Medicare Population

What Medicare Covers

Medicare provides coverage for a wide range of healthcare services, including hospital stays, outpatient care, doctor appointments, and prescription medications (see Figure 2). **There are several options for organizing and funding Medicare benefits:**

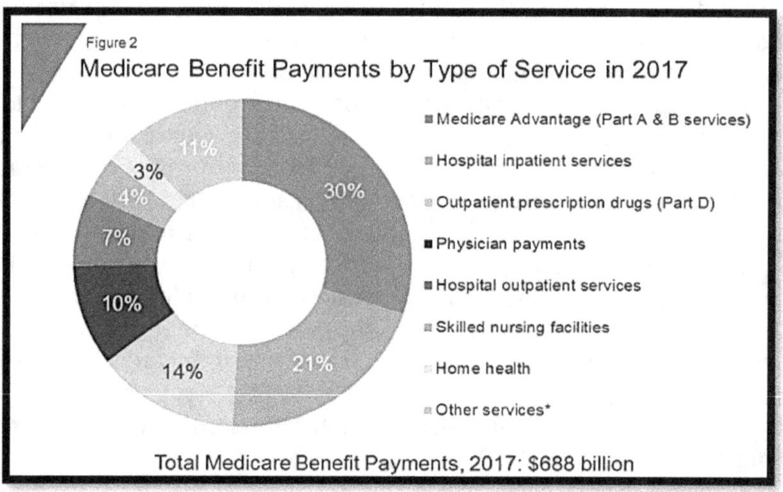

Figure 2: Medicare Benefit Payments by Type of Service in 2017

- **Medicare Part A** primarily provides coverage for services related to inpatient care. This includes hospital stays, skilled nursing facility (SNF) care, hospice care, and certain home health services. It's important to note that while Part A offers comprehensive coverage, beneficiaries are still responsible for certain out-of-pocket costs. For example, in 2019, beneficiaries had to meet a deductible of $1,364 per benefit period, and additional coinsurance payments were required for extended stays. For hospital stays, coinsurance kicks in after 60 days, and for SNF care, after 20 days. Thus, while Part A covers a substantial portion of inpatient services, it is not without its cost-sharing requirements.
- **Medicare Part B** focuses on outpatient services, covering medical treatments outside the hospital, along with some home health care and a range of preventive services. Beneficiaries pay a monthly premium for Part B coverage, and in 2019, there was a $185 deductible for many of the services under Part B. After the deductible, individuals generally pay 20% coinsurance for services such as doctor visits, lab tests, and durable medical equipment. However, preventive services, like screenings for prostate cancer, mammograms, and an annual wellness visit, are often fully covered by Medicare without any out-of-pocket costs for the patient. These services are exempt from cost-sharing if they meet the standards set by the U.S. Preventive Services Task Force with an A or B rating, ensuring that beneficiaries have access to essential preventive care.

- **Medicare Part C**, commonly referred to as Medicare Advantage, provides an alternative way for enrollees to receive their Medicare benefits. Instead of getting services through the traditional Medicare system, individuals can opt to join private health plans, such as Health Maintenance Organizations (HMOs) or Preferred Provider Organizations (PPOs). These plans are required to cover all of the services offered under Parts A and B, and many of them also include additional benefits, such as prescription drug coverage, which is typically associated with Part D. Over recent years, the popularity of Medicare Advantage has steadily increased. By 2018, more than 20 million people, accounting for about 34% of all Medicare enrollees, had chosen Medicare Advantage as their preferred method of receiving Medicare benefits. This growing trend reflects the increasing appeal of the more comprehensive and flexible coverage options provided by Medicare Advantage plans.

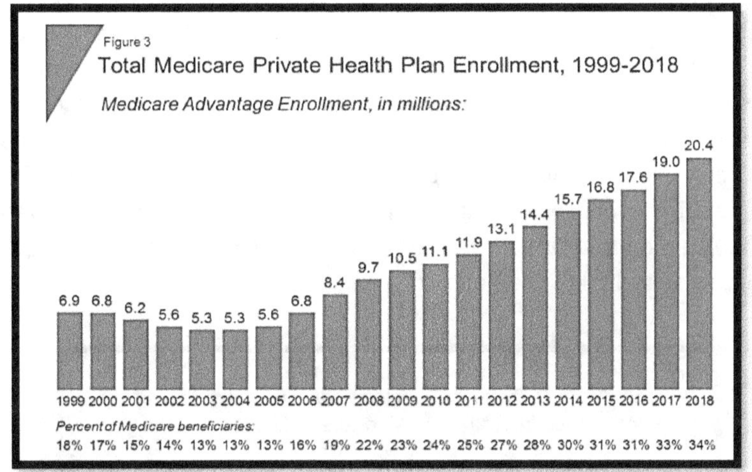

Figure 3: Total Medicare Private Health Plan Enrollment, 1999-2018

Medicare Part D offers prescription drug coverage for beneficiaries, addressing the costs of outpatient medications. This coverage is available through two main options: stand-alone Prescription Drug Plans (PDPs), which work alongside traditional Medicare, and Medicare Advantage plans that include drug coverage (MA-PDs). In 2019, Medicare beneficiaries had access to a variety of choices, including 27 stand-alone PDPs and 21 MA-PDs, allowing individuals to select a plan that best suits their medication needs. One of the primary advantages of Part D is its role in lowering the financial burden of prescription drugs, particularly for high-cost medications. Beneficiaries pay a monthly premium for Part D coverage, but the exact cost can differ depending on the chosen plan and the individual's specific medications. The plan also includes cost-sharing measures, such as copayments or coinsurance, which vary based on the drug tier and whether the drug is generic or brand-name.

For those with limited income or resources, additional financial assistance is available through the Extra Help program, which helps reduce or eliminate premiums, deductibles, and other out-of-pocket expenses. This program is particularly important for low-income seniors, as it ensures they access the medications they need without facing significant financial hardship. By 2018, the number of Medicare beneficiaries enrolled in either a PDP or an MA-PD had grown to 43 million. Of these, around 25% were receiving low-income subsidies, demonstrating the essential role that Medicare Part D plays in providing affordable prescription drugs to millions of Americans. This widespread enrollment highlights the importance of drug coverage in the overall Medicare system, offering critical support for both common and high-cost medications across various income levels.

Benefit Gaps and Supplemental Coverage

Medicare covers the costs of many health care services, but standard Medicare has high deductibles and copayment requirements, and there is no cap on how much Parts A and B recipients can spend out of pocket and still get coverage. Traditional Medicare also doesn't cover some services that are important for older people and people with disabilities. These include long-term care and support, dental care, eyeglasses, and hearing aids. Because Medicare has cost-sharing requirements, benefit gaps, and no yearly out-of-pocket spending cap, most people who are covered by traditional Medicare also have some kind of additional coverage that helps pay for their costs and fill in the benefit gaps (Figure 4).

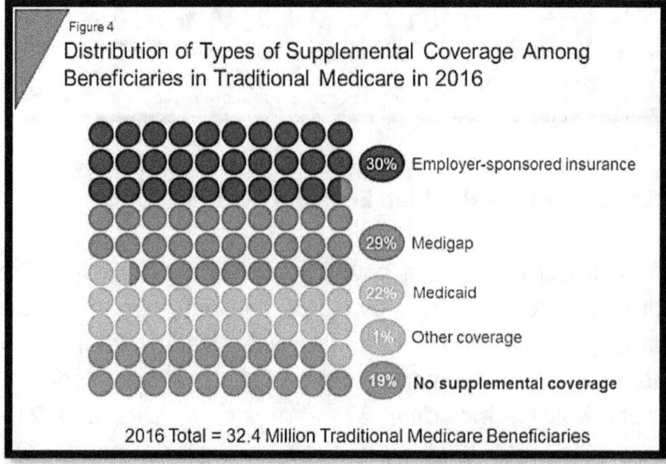

Figure 4: Distribution of Types of Supplemental Coverage Among Beneficiaries in Traditional Medicare, 2016

In 2016, **employer-sponsored insurance** played a significant role in providing retiree health benefits for 30% of individuals enrolled in traditional Medicare. This type of supplemental coverage, often offered through retirees' former employers, helped reduce out-of-pocket costs for these beneficiaries. However, the availability of such benefits has seen a sharp decline over the years. In 1988, approximately 66% of large employers provided retiree health benefits, but by 2018, this percentage had dwindled to just 18%. The shrinking availability of employer-sponsored retiree insurance underscores a growing reliance on alternative forms of supplemental coverage. Around 29% of traditional Medicare enrollees in 2016 purchased **Medigap** policies, also known as Medicare Supplement Insurance. Medigap plans are offered by private insurers and are specifically designed to cover out-of-pocket expenses that Medicare Parts A and B do not fully pay for, such as copayments, coinsurance, and deductibles. This additional coverage helps reduce the financial burden on beneficiaries by covering many of the cost-sharing expenses associated with hospital stays, doctor visits, and other medical services. Medigap plans vary in terms of coverage, with some plans providing more comprehensive benefits than others, giving enrollees options based on their financial needs and medical situations.

For **low-income Medicare beneficiaries**, Medicaid provides vital additional coverage. In 2016, more than 7 million individuals enrolled in traditional Medicare—about 22%—qualified for Medicaid due to their limited incomes and assets. This figure does not include the 3.5 million individuals enrolled in both Medicare Advantage and Medicaid. These beneficiaries, known as **dual-eligibles**, receive benefits from both programs. Of the 7 million dual-eligibles with traditional Medicare, approximately 5.3 million had comprehensive Medicaid coverage, which includes services not covered by Medicare, such as long-term care. Medicaid also covers their Medicare premiums and cost-sharing responsibilities, greatly easing their financial burden. The remaining 1.7 million dual-eligibles receive more limited Medicaid benefits through the **Medicare Savings Programs**, which help pay for Medicare premiums and sometimes cost-sharing expenses, though they do not receive full Medicaid services. On the other hand, 19% of traditional Medicare enrollees, which equates to roughly 6 million people, did not have any form of **supplemental insurance** in 2016. These individuals are responsible for all cost-sharing obligations under Medicare, including deductibles, copayments, and coinsurance, which can lead to significant out-of-pocket spending. Additionally, unlike those enrolled in Medicare Advantage plans, these beneficiaries do not have an annual out-of-pocket spending limit, making it more difficult to manage unexpected medical expenses.

Medicare Advantage

By 2018, around one-third of all Medicare beneficiaries chose to enroll in **Medicare Advantage** plans instead of traditional Medicare. Some of these beneficiaries also had supplemental coverage through Medicaid or employer/union-sponsored plans, further reducing their out-of-pocket costs. Medicare Advantage plans are required to limit in-network out-of-pocket costs for services under Parts A and B to no more than $6,700 per year. Moreover, many Medicare Advantage plans offer extra benefits not covered by traditional Medicare, such as dental care, vision services (including eyeglasses), and hearing aids. These additional services make Medicare

Advantage plans an attractive option for those seeking more comprehensive healthcare coverage.

Medicare Beneficiaries' Out-of-Pocket Healthcare Spending

In 2016, Medicare beneficiaries enrolled in both Part A and Part B under traditional Medicare faced significant out-of-pocket expenses, averaging $5,806 per person annually (see Figure 5). A substantial portion of these costs, about 45%, was allocated to paying Medicare premiums and supplemental insurance premiums, such as Medigap or employer-sponsored insurance. The remaining 55% of the total out-of-pocket spending was directed towards medical services, prescription drugs, and long-term care costs. This breakdown highlights the financial challenges faced by many Medicare beneficiaries, particularly those who rely on traditional Medicare without additional coverage to help mitigate their healthcare expenses.

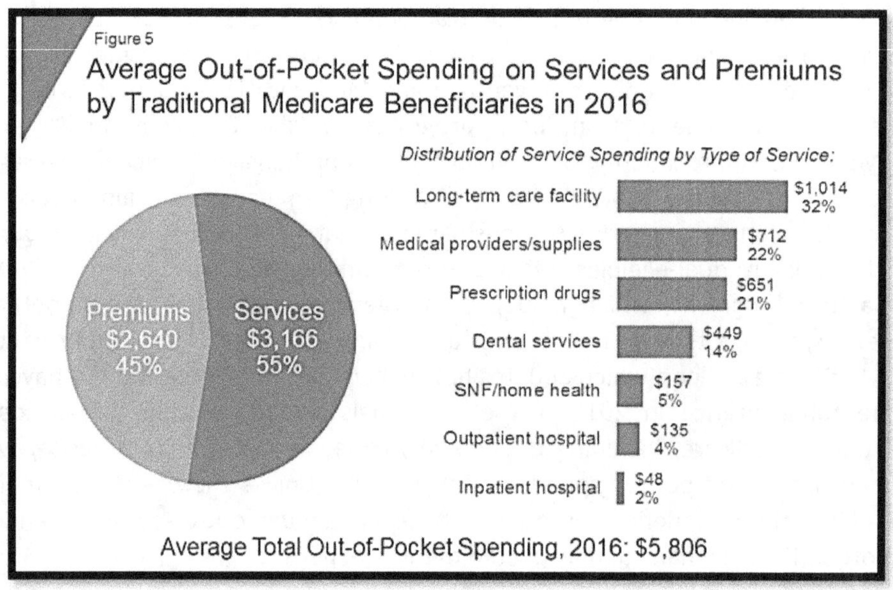

Figure 5: Average Out-of-Pocket Spending on Services and Premiums by Traditional Medicare Beneficiaries in 2016

In 2016, traditional Medicare beneficiaries faced a range of out-of-pocket expenses, with the highest costs associated with **long-term care facilities**. These expenses were followed by payments for medical providers, supplies, prescription medications, and dental services. As beneficiaries age, their healthcare costs typically rise, and this trend is more pronounced among women compared to men. Older women tend to spend more out-of-pocket due to factors such as longer life expectancy and greater healthcare needs. Notably, individuals who reported being in poorer health also incurred higher expenses compared to those who described themselves as healthier. This correlation between health status and out-of-pocket spending reflects the reality that individuals with chronic conditions or other health issues often require more frequent medical care, leading to higher costs over time. The financial burden of these medical expenses can be particularly challenging for older adults, especially those without supplemental coverage to help mitigate out-of-pocket costs.

Medicare Spending: Present and Future Trends

Medicare spending continues to play a critical role in the U.S. healthcare system. In 2017, **total Medicare benefit payments** reached an impressive $688 billion. A significant portion of this, about 21%, was spent on inpatient hospital services, covering treatments for acute conditions that require hospitalization. Another 14% of spending went toward outpatient prescription drugs, reflecting the high cost of medications, especially for those with chronic conditions. Physician services accounted for 10% of Medicare spending, as regular doctor visits and treatments form a key part of healthcare for older adults. In addition to traditional Medicare services, 30% of Medicare's spending in 2017 was directed to **Medicare Advantage plans**, which provide a managed care alternative to traditional Medicare under Parts A and B. These plans are becoming an increasingly popular option for beneficiaries, as they often include additional benefits like vision, dental, and hearing care, along with prescription drug coverage.

Several factors are driving current and future Medicare spending trends. The **number of enrollees** is a primary influence, as the Medicare population continues to grow rapidly with the aging of the baby boomer generation. As more people retire and become eligible for Medicare, overall spending rises. Another key factor is how care is delivered. Shifts toward more expensive forms of care, including specialized treatments and increased prescription drug use, contribute to higher spending. Moreover, the **frequency of services** used by beneficiaries, especially in areas like outpatient care and pharmaceuticals, has increased over time, further elevating costs. Although Medicare spending has seen some moderation in recent years—both on a per-person basis and in total—**future projections** indicate a sharp increase over the coming decade. From $583 billion in 2018, Medicare spending is expected to more than double, reaching an estimated $1.26 trillion by 2028. This projection excludes revenue from premiums and other sources and is driven by several key factors. **Longer life expectancies**, which lead to extended periods of Medicare enrollment, along with the growing number of beneficiaries, will continue to fuel rising costs. Additionally, **rising healthcare costs per individual**, including hospital services, medications, and long-term care, will put further pressure on Medicare's budget.

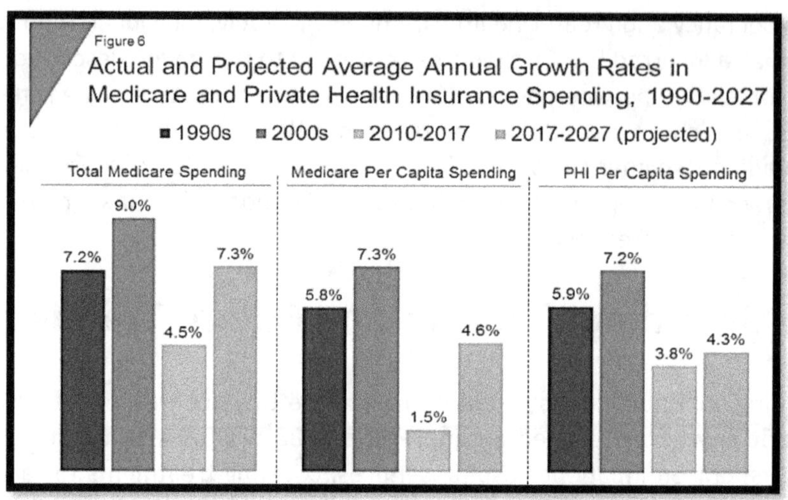

Figure 6: Actual and Projected Average Annual Growth Rates in Medicare and Private Health Insurance Spending, 1990-2027

One of the most significant concerns surrounding **Medicare spending** is the rapid rise in prescription drug costs, particularly within the **Part D prescription drug program**. Over the next decade, the cost of providing prescription drug coverage through Part D is expected to increase at a faster rate, with annual growth projected at 4.6%. This marks a notable acceleration compared to the period between 2010 and 2017, when Part D costs grew at an average annual rate of 2.2% (see Figure 7). A major factor contributing to this anticipated increase is the rising cost of **specialty drugs**, which are typically used to treat complex or chronic conditions such as cancer, autoimmune diseases, and rare genetic disorders. These medications often come with high price tags due to the advanced technology and research required to develop them, as well as limited competition in the marketplace. As more Medicare beneficiaries rely on these expensive treatments, the overall cost burden on the Part D program continues to grow. In addition to the rising prices of individual medications, the **increased use of specialty drugs** within the Medicare population is also contributing to higher spending. These drugs are becoming more commonly prescribed as new treatments are developed and more patients are diagnosed with conditions that require them. As a result, even with measures in place to negotiate prices or manage costs, the financial demands on Medicare Part D are expected to escalate in the coming years. Efforts to control rising drug costs are ongoing, but the projected growth in spending highlights the challenges Medicare faces in balancing the need to provide beneficiaries with access to cutting-edge treatments while managing the sustainability of the program. The increasing reliance on expensive medications will likely remain a key issue for Medicare policymakers in the foreseeable future.

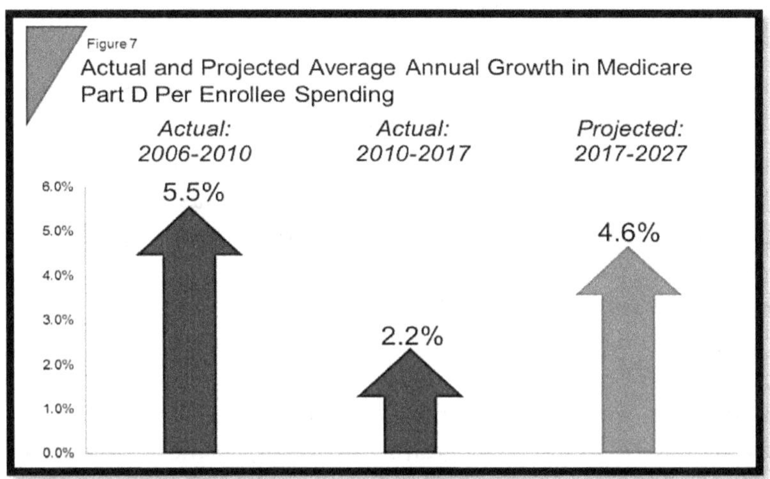

Figure 7: Actual and Projected Average Annual Growth in Medicare Part D Per Enrollee Spending

How Medicare is financed

Figure 8 shows that Medicare is paid for by general revenues (41% in 2017), payroll tax contributions (37%), beneficiary fees (14%), and other sources.

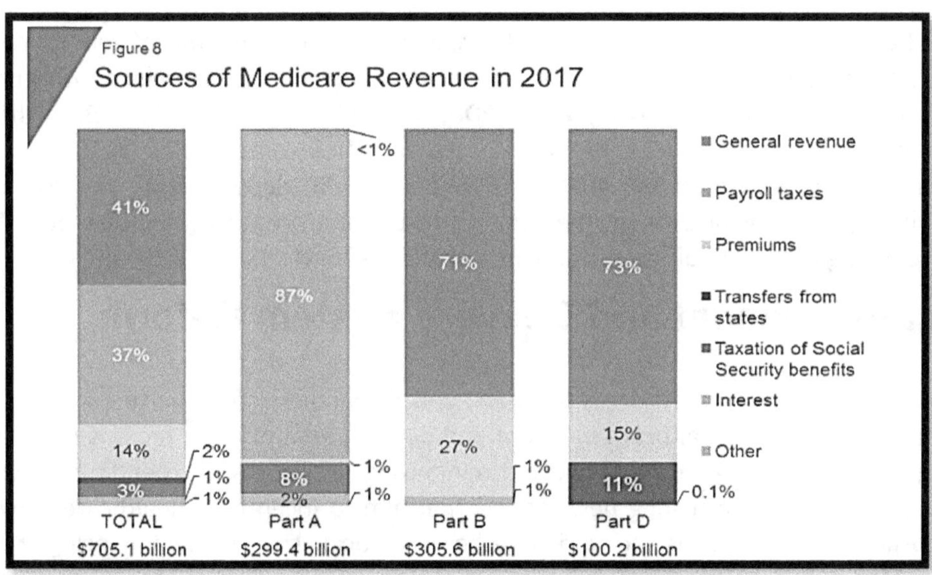

Figure 8: Sources of Medicare Revenue in 2017

Medicare Part A, which covers hospital insurance, is primarily financed through a payroll tax. Employers and employees equally share this 2.9% tax, which is deposited into the Hospital Insurance (HI) Trust Fund. This fund is used to cover the costs of inpatient hospital care, skilled nursing facility care, and some home health services. For higher-income earners—those with individual incomes exceeding $200,000 or joint incomes above $250,000—the payroll tax rate increases to 2.35%. Despite these contributions, the financial sustainability of the Part A Trust Fund remains a concern, as it is projected to become insolvent by 2026 unless significant changes are made.

Medicare Part B, which provides coverage for outpatient services such as doctor visits, medical supplies, and preventive services, is funded through a combination of general tax revenues and monthly premiums paid by beneficiaries. In 2019, the standard monthly premium for Part B was $135.50. For beneficiaries with lower incomes who qualify for Medicaid, these premiums are covered through federal assistance programs. However, higher-income individuals—those earning more than $85,000 per year (or $170,000 for couples)—are required to pay an income-adjusted premium. This premium can range from $189.60 to $460.50 per month in 2019, depending on income levels, covering between 35% and 85% of total Part B costs.

Medicare Part C, also known as **Medicare Advantage**, does not have a separate funding mechanism, as it is integrated with Parts A, B, and sometimes D. The funding for Medicare Advantage comes from the same sources—payroll taxes, beneficiary premiums, and general revenues. Enrollees in Medicare Advantage plans typically pay the standard Part B premium, and many plans also require an additional premium for the extra benefits they offer. In 2018, the average monthly premium for a Medicare Advantage plan that included prescription drug coverage was $34. However, these costs can vary widely depending on the plan and the services provided.

Medicare Part D, which covers prescription drugs, is funded through a mix of general revenues, state contributions, and premiums paid by beneficiaries. In 2018, the average monthly premium for a stand-alone **Prescription Drug Plan (PDP)** was $41. Similar to Part B, high-income beneficiaries must pay an additional premium based on their income level. In 2019, this income-related premium ranged from $12.40 to $77.40 per month, depending on the beneficiary's income. These premiums help offset the cost of prescription drugs for Medicare beneficiaries, but the increasing cost of medications remains a challenge for the Part D program.

Medicare Payment and Delivery System Reform

Policymakers, healthcare professionals, insurers, and researchers continue to explore different approaches for reforming healthcare payment and delivery systems. The focus is on addressing escalating costs, improving care quality, and minimizing unnecessary expenditures. Medicare has taken a leading role in testing new models that aim to incentivize healthcare providers—such as hospitals and physicians—to work together in reducing costs while enhancing the quality of care for Medicare beneficiaries. These reforms aim to link a portion of Medicare payments to the value of care provided, which is evaluated based on providers' success in meeting specific goals related to cost control and care quality. One of the key models being tested within

Medicare is the **Accountable Care Organization (ACO)** model. In 2018, over 10 million Medicare beneficiaries were enrolled in ACOs. The ACO model allows groups of healthcare providers to assume collective responsibility for the overall care of their Medicare patients. Providers in ACOs share in financial rewards if they successfully meet predetermined benchmarks for reducing costs and improving care quality. Conversely, they may also share in financial losses if they fail to meet these targets. This model encourages collaboration among providers to deliver more coordinated and efficient care.

In addition to ACOs, Medicare is experimenting with other payment models, such as **medical homes**, which provide a patient-centered approach to primary care, and **bundled payment initiatives**. Bundled payments consolidate payments to multiple providers involved in a single episode of care, such as a surgery, encouraging providers to coordinate their efforts and reduce unnecessary services. Another key initiative focuses on reducing **hospital readmissions**, which aims to prevent patients from being readmitted to the hospital after their initial discharge through better post-hospital care and follow-up services. Many of these payment reform models are overseen by the **Center for Medicare and Medicaid Innovation (CMMI)**, which was established under the Affordable Care Act (ACA). CMMI is tasked with testing and evaluating these models to assess their effectiveness in lowering costs and improving care. If a model is shown to improve care quality without increasing costs, or if it reduces costs without compromising the quality of care, the Secretary of Health and Human Services (HHS) has the authority to expand or extend the model on a broader scale.

Looking to the Future

Medicare faces a number of significant challenges, with one of the most pressing being how to ensure older adults have access to affordable, high-quality care, while maintaining the financial sustainability of the program for future generations. Although Medicare spending has recently been growing at a slower rate compared to previous decades, there are signs that both total and per capita spending are beginning to increase again, gradually rising from the historically low levels seen in recent years. One area of particular concern is the escalating cost of prescription drugs. The **Medicare Trustees** project that spending on **Part D**, which covers prescription drugs, will grow faster on a per-person basis in the coming years, driven largely by the increasing cost of specialty medications that treat complex and chronic conditions. In addition to rising prescription drug costs, the aging of the population presents another substantial challenge. As the number of people entering retirement age continues to grow, there is increasing pressure on Medicare's ability to fund healthcare for a larger portion of the population. To address these challenges, various policy changes have been proposed. Some suggestions include restructuring Medicare's **benefits and cost-sharing** mechanisms, raising the **eligibility age** for Medicare, transitioning from a **defined benefit** system (where specific benefits are guaranteed) to a **premium support model** (where beneficiaries receive a fixed amount to purchase coverage), and even allowing people under 65 to **buy into Medicare**.

When considering these proposed reforms, it is crucial for policymakers to weigh their potential effects on several key areas: overall healthcare costs, Medicare's financial outlook, beneficiaries' access to care, and the affordability of coverage. Any significant changes to the program must take into account how they will impact the availability and quality of care for Medicare recipients, as well as how many beneficiaries will be expected to pay out of pocket. Ensuring that Medicare remains a reliable source of affordable healthcare for older adults while addressing the growing financial strain on the program will require thoughtful and balanced policy decisions.

Who is Eligible for Medicare?

Many things decide if someone is eligible for Medicare, but the main ones are age, work experience, disability status, or certain medical conditions. People must fit into one of the following groups to be eligible for Medicare. **Here is a more detailed list of people who can get Medicare:**

1. **Individuals Aged 65 and Older**

Most people who are eligible for Medicare do so when they turn 65. **In this age group, there are, however, some extra conditions and requirements that must be met:**

- o **Citizenship and Residency:** People who are citizens or legal permanent residents of the United States can get Medicare. Legal residents must have stayed in the U.S. for at least five years straight before asking for Medicare to be eligible.
- o **Work History Requirements for Premium-Free Part A:** Part A of Medicare covers hospital care and is usually offered for free to people who have worked and paid Medicare taxes for a long time. In particular, people (or their wives) must have worked at a job that withheld Medicare taxes for at least 40 quarters, which is equal to 10 years. People who haven't earned enough work points can still get Part A coverage, but they will have to pay a monthly premium.
- o **Part B Enrollment:** Most people can get Part A without paying a premium, but everyone who signs up for Part B have to pay a monthly premium. Part B covers outpatient care, doctor visits, and preventive care. Part B is optional, but it's often necessary to cover medical care that doesn't happen in a hospital. A lot of people who turn 65 and sign up for Medicare do so for both Parts A and B.

2. **People Under 65 with Disabilities**

Medicare isn't exclusively for individuals aged 65 and older; it also extends to millions of younger people with disability. If you're under 65 and qualify for Medicare, there are specific pathways that may grant you access to the program. **Here are the primary ways this can happen:**

- **Social Security Disability Insurance (SSDI) Recipients:** Individuals under the age of 65 who have been receiving SSDI benefits for a minimum of 24 months become eligible for Medicare. Unfortunately, during this 24-month waiting period, many are left without sufficient health coverage unless they have other forms of insurance. Once the waiting period ends, they can take full advantage of Medicare, gaining access to the same coverage options available to those over 65, including hospital, medical, and prescription drug benefits.

- **Medicare for ALS (Amyotrophic Lateral Sclerosis) Patients:** Commonly known as Lou Gehrig's disease, ALS is a progressive neurological condition affecting the brain and spinal cord. For those diagnosed with ALS, the Medicare eligibility process is expedited. As soon as individuals begin receiving SSDI benefits, they can immediately enroll in Medicare without having to wait the usual 24 months required for most other conditions. This ensures that patients have access to essential healthcare services without unnecessary delays, which is especially critical for managing the complexities of ALS.

These exceptions are in place to help ensure that those who are most vulnerable due to severe disabilities or debilitating conditions have timely access to healthcare coverage when they need it the most.

3. **People with End-Stage Renal Disease (ESRD)**

Medicare has special rules for people who have very bad kidney problems:

- **Definition and Coverage:** End-stage renal disease (ESRD) is a situation in which the kidneys have stopped working completely and need to be treated regularly with dialysis or a kidney donation is needed. Anyone with ESRD can get Medicare, no matter what age they are. Insurance starts to pay for dialysis on the first day of the fourth month, or earlier if the person knows how to do it on their own at home or has had a kidney donation.
- **Eligibility Criteria for ESRD:** People with ESRD can get Medicare coverage if they meet certain requirements, such as having enough work experience (or being the spouse or child of someone who does) or already getting SSDI or railroad retirement benefits.

4. **Spouse and Dependent Eligibility**

Sometimes, partners or dependents can get Medicare too, even if they don't meet the work history standards on their own:

- **Spousal Eligibility:** If one partner has met the work history requirements for Medicare (i.e., paid Medicare taxes for 40 quarters), the other spouse may be able to get Part A for free when they turn 65, even if they have never worked before. There are times when this rule applies even if one partner didn't work or didn't have a job that paid Medicare taxes.
- **Divorced or Widowed Spouses:** If you were married for at least 10 years to someone who meets Medicare's work standards, you may also be able to get Medicare benefits based on your work history. This is true whether the person is divorced or dead, and they can keep getting the benefits as long as they are not married when they sign up.
- **Medicare for Dependent Children:** Dependent children may be able to get Medicare if they meet certain requirements because of a disability or medical condition (like ESRD) or if they are the dependents of someone qualified for Medicare because of a disability or work experience.

5. **Enrolling in Medicare**

For those nearing Medicare eligibility, understanding the enrollment process is essential to avoid any potential penalties or lapses in coverage. **Here are the main ways to sign up for Medicare:**

- **Initial Enrollment Period (IEP):** When approaching your 65th birthday, you have a specific seven-month window to enroll in Medicare, known as the Initial Enrollment Period. This period starts three months before the month you turn 65, includes your birthday month, and extends for another three months afterward. It's critical to sign up during this time to avoid late enrollment penalties. Missing the IEP could result in higher premiums for Part B (medical insurance) and Part D (prescription drug coverage), which may last for as long as you remain on Medicare.
- **Automatic Enrollment for Some Beneficiaries:** If you've already been receiving Social Security or Railroad Retirement Board benefits for at least four months before your 65th birthday, you'll typically be automatically enrolled in both Medicare Part A (hospital insurance) and Part B (medical insurance). While this automatic enrollment helps simplify the process, it's important to review your Medicare coverage options, as some individuals might prefer to delay Part B due to other health insurance coverage. If you're not automatically enrolled, you'll need to sign up manually through the Social Security Administration.
- **Special Enrollment Periods (SEPs):** For those who continue to work beyond age 65 or have health insurance through their employer or spouse's job, there's an option to delay enrolling in Medicare without incurring a penalty. When your employment or coverage ends, you will have an eight-month Special Enrollment Period to sign up for Medicare without facing late penalties. It's important to note that this period starts when the employment or group health plan coverage ends, not when COBRA or retiree coverage ends, so careful timing is key to avoiding gaps in healthcare coverage.

Knowing these different enrollment periods can help you plan ahead and ensure you don't miss out on Medicare benefits when you become eligible.

CHAPTER 2

UNDERSTANDING MEDICARE PARTS

Medicare Part A (Hospital Insurance)

Some people have to pay a premium for this part, but most people get it for free. To get Part A for free, a person must be qualified for Medicare because of their earnings or the earnings of a husband, parent, or child; they need to have met a certain number of coverage periods (QCs) and apply for Social Security or Railroad Retirement Board (RRB) benefits. If the person is applying for Part A because of age, disability, or End Stage Renal Disease (ESRD), they will need a different number of QCs. While employed, individuals contribute payroll taxes through the Federal Insurance Contributions Act (FICA), which allows them to earn quarters of coverage (QCs). These QCs typically help qualify people for both monthly Social Security benefits and premium-free Medicare Part A, as they pay the full FICA tax. **Note:** Certain employees of federal, state, or local governments only contribute to the Part A portion of the FICA tax. The QCs they accumulate can only be applied toward meeting the criteria for premium-free Part A, but they do not count toward eligibility for monthly Social Security benefits.

Premium-Free Medicare Part A Based on Age

To qualify for Medicare Part A without paying premiums, individuals must meet certain age and eligibility requirements:
- **Eligibility Criteria**: The individual must be at least 65 years of age and be eligible for monthly cash benefits from either Social Security or the Railroad Retirement Board (RRB).
- **Automatic Enrollment**: If someone has been receiving Social Security or RRB benefits for at least four months before their 65th birthday, they are automatically enrolled in Medicare Part A. No additional application is necessary, and their Medicare coverage begins when they turn 65.
- **Manual Enrollment**: For those not receiving Social Security or RRB benefits yet, they must apply for Medicare through the Social Security Administration. If they apply for Part A (or Social Security or RRB benefits) within six months of turning 65, Medicare coverage will begin the month they turn 65, as long as they apply during that month. If someone delays applying for more than six months after turning 65, their Part A coverage will be retroactive for up to six months.
- **Special Case for Early Birthdays**: If an individual's birthday falls on the first day of the month, their Medicare Part A coverage begins one month earlier. For instance, someone born on December 1 will have their Medicare coverage start on November 1.

Medicare Part A Based on Age for Those Who Must Pay a Premium

For individuals who do not qualify for premium-free Part A, the process requires extra steps:
- **Manual Enrollment**: Those who must pay for Part A are not automatically enrolled in Medicare at age 65. They must proactively contact the Social Security Administration and apply for enrollment during an appropriate enrollment period. Additionally, they must already be enrolled in or sign up for Part B (medical insurance).
- **Premium Payments**: Both Part A and Part B premiums must be paid on time to maintain Medicare coverage. Failure to do so could lead to losing coverage.
- **Coverage Start**: Once enrolled, Medicare Part A coverage for those paying a premium begins the month following their enrollment.

Medicare Eligibility Based on Disability

Individuals receiving monthly disability benefits through Social Security or the Railroad Retirement Board (RRB) are automatically eligible for Medicare Part A after receiving those benefits for 24 months. This rule also applies to federal, state, and local government employees who may not qualify for Social Security but receive disability benefits. **After 29 months of disability, these workers also automatically qualify for Medicare Part A.**
- **Special Rule for ALS (Amyotrophic Lateral Sclerosis)**: Individuals diagnosed with ALS, also known as Lou Gehrig's disease, are eligible for Medicare Part A as soon as they begin receiving disability payments from Social Security or the RRB. They do not have to wait the typical 24 months to receive Medicare benefits, ensuring immediate access to critical care.
- **Child Disability Benefits**: Under the Social Security Administration (SSA) guidelines, children cannot receive disability payments until they reach 18 years of age. Consequently, Medicare Part A benefits related to child disability claims cannot begin before the individual turns 20 (or 18 in the case of ALS patients).

Medicare for End-Stage Renal Disease (ESRD)

Individuals diagnosed with End-Stage Renal Disease (ESRD) are eligible for premium-free Medicare Part A if they meet certain conditions. **This applies to those receiving dialysis or who have undergone a kidney transplant. Qualification criteria include:**
- **Eligibility**: Individuals must have worked the required number of years under Social Security, the RRB, or as a government employee, or be eligible for or receiving Social Security or RRB benefits. Spouses and dependent children of individuals who meet these work requirements may also qualify for Medicare Part A coverage.
- **When Coverage Starts**: Coverage typically begins:
  - The third month after starting regular dialysis, or
  - The first month of daily dialysis if the individual learns to perform it independently, or
  - The month of the kidney transplant, or

o   Two months before the transplant month if the individual was hospitalized to prepare for the procedure.

Medicare Part B (Medical Insurance)

Medicare Part B covers medical services such as doctor visits, outpatient care, and preventive services. Most individuals in the U.S. who have been receiving Social Security or RRB benefits for at least four months before their Medicare eligibility date are automatically enrolled in both Medicare Parts A and B, with Part B requiring a monthly premium. **This automatic enrollment can be accepted or declined.**
- **Puerto Rico Residents**: Those residing in Puerto Rico who are eligible for automatic Medicare enrollment only receive Part A automatically. They must manually sign up for Part B if they wish to receive its benefits.
- **Manual Enrollment**: Individuals who are not receiving Social Security or RRB benefits or who previously declined Part B must manually enroll during specific enrollment periods to avoid penalties. A late enrollment penalty applies to individuals who delay signing up for Part B beyond their Initial Enrollment Period (IEP), resulting in higher premiums for as long as they have Part B coverage.
- **Eligibility for Part B**: To enroll in Medicare Part B, individuals must:
  - Be at least 65 years old,
  - Live in the U.S.,
  - Be either a U.S. citizen or a legal permanent resident who has resided in the country for at least five continuous years before applying for Medicare.

In certain cases, individuals who have lost Part A coverage due to a kidney transplant may still qualify for the Part B Immunosuppressive Drug benefit.

Medicare Enrollment Periods and Coverage Start

To enroll in Medicare Part A or B, individuals who are not automatically enrolled must apply during specific enrollment periods. These periods include:
- **Initial Enrollment Period (IEP)**: The seven-month window around your 65th birthday.
- **General Enrollment Period (GEP)**: Held annually from January 1 to March 31 for those who missed their IEP.
- **Special Enrollment Period (SEP)**: Available to individuals who delay Medicare enrollment due to current employment or other qualifying coverage.

By understanding these enrollment periods, individuals can ensure timely access to Medicare and avoid potential penalties.

Initial Enrollment Period (IEP)

The Initial Enrollment Period (IEP) provides a seven-month window for individuals to enroll in Medicare when they first become eligible. This period starts three months before the month of their 65th birthday and ends three months after. During this time, those turning 65 can sign up for Medicare without facing late penalties. For individuals under 65 who qualify due to a disability, Medicare enrollment begins after they have received disability benefits for 25 months. In these cases, their IEP begins three months before their 25th month of receiving disability benefits and continues for three months after. It's important to note that individuals with End-Stage Renal Disease (ESRD) or Amyotrophic Lateral Sclerosis (ALS) have their own distinct IEPs, tailored to their specific health conditions. When someone enrolls in Medicare during their IEP, their coverage typically begins the month after enrollment. For disabled individuals, automatic enrollment in Medicare Parts A and B occurs after they have been receiving Social Security disability benefits for 24 months. Failure to enroll in Medicare Part B or premium-based Part A during the IEP often results in a late enrollment penalty, with the Part B penalty continuing for as long as the individual has Part B coverage.

General Enrollment Period (GEP)

The General Enrollment Period (GEP) takes place each year from January 1 to March 31. This period allows individuals who missed their IEP to sign up for Medicare. Coverage for Medicare Part B and premium-based Part A begins in the month following their enrollment during the GEP. It is important to use this period if you missed your initial opportunity, though late penalties may still apply.

Special Enrollment Period (SEP)

The Special Enrollment Period (SEP) allows individuals to sign up for Medicare Part B and premium-based Part A without incurring late penalties, but these enrollment windows are only available under specific conditions. For example, individuals who delay enrolling in Medicare due to having qualifying employer-based health coverage can use an SEP to avoid penalties. If someone misses their SEP, they must wait until the next GEP to enroll, which could leave them without coverage and subject them to penalties.

SEP for the Working Aged and Working Disabled

Those who are still covered by a group health plan through their employer or their spouse's job can delay signing up for Medicare when they first become eligible. Individuals with disabilities who are covered by a family member's group health plan also qualify for this SEP. These individuals can enroll in Medicare at any time while they are still covered by the employer's group health plan, or during the eight months after employment or group coverage ends, whichever occurs first. However, individuals with ESRD are not eligible to use this SEP to enroll in Medicare.

SEP for International Volunteers

This SEP applies to individuals who did not enroll in Medicare Part A or Part B when first eligible because they were volunteering outside the U.S. for at least 12 months with a tax-exempt organization. To qualify, they must have had health coverage during their time abroad. **This SEP lasts for six months, beginning the first day of the month after any of the following events:**
- The individual stops volunteering abroad.
- The organization's tax-exempt status ends.
- The volunteer no longer has health coverage while overseas.

SEP for Certain TRICARE Beneficiaries

This SEP is for individuals under 65 who are entitled to TRICARE due to disability or ESRD but did not enroll in Medicare Part B because of their TRICARE coverage. Eligible individuals include retired military members, their family members, or those on active duty who qualify for Medicare because of ESRD. The SEP allows enrollment either during or after the IEP, if the person was informed of their Medicare eligibility during this time. Coverage begins either the month of enrollment, the month following enrollment, or the month after Part B coverage was terminated due to refusal. For ESRD cases, coverage begins based on the month of Part A entitlement, the enrollment month, or the month after the IEP ends.

SEP for Exceptional Conditions (Effective January 1, 2023)

As of 2023, new SEPs are available for Medicare enrollment in special circumstances. These SEPs are designed to accommodate individuals who were unable to enroll due to extraordinary situations.

SEP for Individuals Affected by an Emergency or Disaster

Individuals who did not sign up for Medicare Part A or Part B when first eligible due to a federal, state, or locally declared emergency or disaster can take advantage of this SEP. It applies to those affected by such events, allowing them to enroll for up to six months after the disaster ends. This also applies if the emergency affected the person's legal guardian, authorized agent, or healthcare decision-maker. **The SEP starts on the date the emergency is declared and ends six months after the later of the following:**
- The official end of the emergency,
- The expiration or revocation of the emergency declaration, or
- The date the declaration was made if it occurred after the event ended.

Medicare coverage will start the first day of the month following enrollment.

SEP for Misrepresentation by Health Plan or Employer

This SEP applies to individuals who didn't enroll in Medicare Part A or Part B because of incorrect information provided by their employer, group health plan (GHP), or an agent/broker. Individuals must provide proof or a written statement showing that they did not enroll due to misleading advice regarding Medicare enrollment or premium payments. Once notified, the SEP lasts for six months, with Medicare coverage starting the month after enrollment.

Special Enrollment Period (SEP) for Formerly Incarcerated Individuals

Individuals who were incarcerated at the time they first became eligible for Medicare Part B or premium-based Part A have a specific SEP available to them upon release. **This SEP allows them to enroll in Medicare without facing late penalties, provided they apply within the appropriate timeframe.**
- **Eligibility Window**: The SEP begins the day of the individual's release from incarceration and remains open for 12 months, ending on the last day of the 12th month following release.
- **Retroactive Coverage**: Individuals can choose to have their Medicare coverage be retroactive, though it cannot start before their release or extend more than six months into the past. If they opt for retroactive coverage, they are responsible for paying Medicare premiums from the chosen coverage start date.
- **Coverage Start**: If the individual opts not to enroll retroactively, their Medicare benefits will begin on the first day of the month after they enroll.

SEP to Coordinate with Termination of Medicaid Coverage

This SEP is designed for individuals who have lost Medicaid coverage, ensuring that they can enroll in Medicare Part B or premium-based Part A without penalty.
- **Eligibility Window**: The SEP starts when the individual receives notification that their Medicaid coverage is ending and extends for six months from that date.
- **Retroactive Coverage Option**: Individuals may choose to have their Medicare coverage begin retroactively to the first day of the month when they lost Medicaid coverage. If they choose this option, they must pay Medicare premiums dating back to that month.
- **Important Note**: This SEP is only available to those who have lost all Medicaid coverage. Individuals who are still eligible for Medicaid or are part of a Medicare Savings Program are not qualified for this SEP.

SEP for Other Exceptional Conditions

There are certain rare circumstances where individuals may qualify for a Special Enrollment Period (SEP) if they missed their original Medicare enrollment due to reasons beyond their control. These situations must involve specific events that occurred on or after January 1, 2023, and the individual must provide sufficient proof that they could not enroll during their Initial Enrollment Period (IEP) or another enrollment period.

- **Eligibility Criteria**: Individuals must present a written statement or other documentation proving that their missed enrollment was due to an uncontrollable event, such as a severe personal hardship or administrative error.
- **Exclusions**: This SEP does not apply to those who missed enrollment because they were unaware of the program or forgot about the deadline. The Social Security Administration (SSA) will determine eligibility on a case-by-case basis.
- **Enrollment Window**: The SEP will last for a minimum of six months once granted, and Medicare coverage will begin on the first day of the month following enrollment.

Medicare Part A and B Enrollment Forms

Here are the various forms that individuals must complete to enroll in Medicare:

- **CMS-18-F-5**: This form is used to enroll in Medicare Part A for individuals who do not automatically receive it. It can also be used to apply for Part B.
- **CMS-40B**: This form is for those who already have Part A but need to enroll in Part B. For individuals applying under the SEP for the Working Aged and Working Disabled, form CMS-L564 should be submitted alongside it.
- **CMS-4040**: This is used by individuals who are not entitled to Social Security or Railroad Retirement Board benefits but want to enroll in Part B.
- **CMS-43**: Individuals with End-Stage Renal Disease (ESRD) should use this form to enroll in Medicare Parts A and B.
- **CMS-10797**: This form is for individuals eligible for a Special Enrollment Period for premium-based Parts A and B due to specific exceptional circumstances.
- **CMS-L564**: This form should accompany the appropriate enrollment forms when applying for Medicare through the SEP for the Working Aged and Working Disabled.

Termination of Medicare Enrollment

While most individuals cannot voluntarily terminate their Medicare Part A coverage, certain situations can result in the end of Part A or Part B benefits.

- **Premium-Free Part A**: This coverage typically cannot be voluntarily terminated as it is tied to entitlement through Social Security or Railroad Retirement Board benefits. Premium-free Part A usually ends when someone loses their entitlement to those benefits or in the event of death. Specific rules apply for individuals with ESRD, determining when their premium-free Part A ends.
- **Premium-Based Part A and Part B**: These coverage's can be terminated voluntarily. Reasons include failure to pay premiums, a formal request for disenrollment, or loss of eligibility for Part A in the case of individuals under 65 with a disability or ESRD.
  - **Voluntary Termination**: Individuals who wish to terminate their premium-based Part A and Part B coverage must complete form CMS-1763, which formally requests disenrollment.

Medicare Premiums and Late Enrollment Penalties

- **Income-Related Monthly Adjustment Amount (IRMAA)**: Some Medicare beneficiaries with higher incomes are required to pay an additional amount on top of their regular Medicare premiums for Part B and Part D. This adjustment affects less than 5% of Medicare recipients.
- **Late Enrollment Penalty (LEP) for Premium-Based Part A**: Individuals who delay enrolling in premium-based Part A when first eligible may face a penalty. The Part A premium can increase by up to 10%, and the individual will be required to pay this higher premium for twice the number of years they delayed enrollment. However, individuals using the SEP for the Working Aged and Working Disabled are subject to different rules when calculating this penalty. For them, the penalty is determined by counting the months between the end of their IEP and the date of their enrollment, excluding months in which they had group health coverage.
    - **Exceptions**: No LEP applies to individuals using the SEP for Exceptional Conditions or the SEP for International Volunteers.
- **Late Enrollment Penalty (LEP) for Part B**: Individuals who do not enroll in Part B when first eligible are also subject to a penalty. The Part B premium increases by 10% for each 12-month period during which the individual was eligible but did not enroll. This penalty lasts for as long as the individual has Medicare.
    - **Special Circumstances**: No LEP applies to individuals using the SEP for Exceptional Conditions, International Volunteers, or Certain TRICARE Beneficiaries.

Medicare Part C (Medicare Advantage)

Another way to get your Medicare benefits is through Medicare Part C, which is also called **Medicare Advantage.** It is given by private insurance companies that Medicare has accepted. If you sign up for a Medicare Advantage plan, you will still have Medicare. However, your Medicare Part A (hospital insurance) and Part B (medical insurance) coverage will not come straight from the federal government, but from the private insurance plan.

What Medicare Part C (Medicare Advantage) Covers

1. **Core Medicare Benefits (Required Coverage)**

All of the services that Original Medicare covers must be offered by Medicare Advantage plans. This means that if you sign up for a Medicare Advantage plan, you will still get the same hospital and medical treatment as under Medicare Parts A and B. The main benefits are:

Part A (Hospital Insurance) Coverage in Medicare Advantage

- **Inpatient Hospital Care:** This covers a semi-private room, meals, general nursing care, and hospital services for stays in critical access hospitals, acute care hospitals, long-term care hospitals, and mental health inpatient hospitals.
- **Skilled Nursing Facility (SNF) Care:** Medicare Advantage plans cover the same benefits for skilled nursing care as Original Medicare. This includes short-term stays after a hospital stay if medically necessary.
- **Home Health Care:** This includes some limited home health services for people who are getting better after being sick or hurt, like physical therapy or part-time nursing care.
- **Hospice Care:** Hospice care is still covered by Original Medicare, even for people who have Medicare Advantage. However, Medicare Advantage plans may help organize care and offer extra benefits for end-of-life care.

Part B (Medical Insurance) Coverage in Medicare Advantage

- **Doctor Visits and Outpatient Services:** Medicare Advantage plans cover all medically necessary services given by doctors and specialists. This includes visits to the doctor, outpatient care, and prevention services like health checks, tests, and vaccines.
- **Diagnostic Tests:** X-rays, MRIs, CT scans, lab tests, and other diagnostic services needed to keep an eye on or figure out health problems are covered.
- **Durable Medical Equipment (DME):** This includes wheelchairs, walkers, oxygen equipment, and other long-lasting medical gear that a doctor recommends.
- **Mental Health Services:** This includes both outpatient and inpatient mental health care. Outpatient mental health care includes visits to therapists or psychologists.
- **Preventive Services:** All preventive services covered by Medicare are given at no cost to people who are enrolled in Medicare Advantage plans. In this group are cancer screenings, vaccines, diabetes screenings, heart tests, and more.

2. **Additional Benefits Beyond Original Medicare**

One of the best things about Medicare Advantage is that many plans give extra benefits that aren't part of Original Medicare. **These are some of the most popular things that Medicare Advantage offers:**

Prescription Drug Coverage (Part D)

Most Medicare Advantage plans cover prescription drugs, which is why they are called **Medicare Advantage Prescription Drug (MAPD)** plans. This means you don't have to sign up for a different Part D plan for prescription drugs. Medicare Advantage plans usually follow a schedule, which is a list of drugs that are covered. Medications are also put into different levels, which can change how much you have to pay out of pocket.

Vision Care

There are a lot of Medicare Advantage plans that cover regular eye care, but Original Medicare does not. Among these are:
- Annual eye exams.
- Coverage for eyeglasses or contact lenses.
- Discounts or full coverage for prescription eyewear.

Hearing Care

A lot of the time, Medicare Advantage plans cover hearing services that Medicare does not. Among these are:
- Routine hearing exams.
- Hearing aid fittings.
- Partial or full coverage for hearing aids, which can be expensive out of pocket under Original Medicare.

Dental Care

Original Medicare doesn't usually cover regular dental care, but many Medicare Advantage plans offer:
- Coverage for preventive dental services such as cleanings, X-rays, and oral exams.
- Coverage for more complex dental procedures, such as fillings, root canals, dentures, and crowns, depends on the plan.

Wellness and Fitness Programs

A lot of Medicare Advantage plans have fitness programs to help people live better lives. Some of these are:
- Memberships to fitness programs such as **SilverSneakers** or **Silver&Fit**, which provide access to gyms and fitness facilities at little to no cost.
- Programs that offer exercise classes specifically designed for seniors.
- Wellness counseling or weight management services.

Over-the-Counter (OTC) Benefits

Some plans give their users a certain amount of allowance that they can spend on over-the-counter medicines and health-related items, like
- Vitamins and supplements.
- Bandages, pain relievers, and other common OTC medications.
- Personal care items like toothpaste, skin creams, and more.

Transportation Services

Some Medicare Advantage plans cover rides to and from medical visits that aren't emergencies. This can be very helpful for people who need help getting to regular therapy sessions, doctor visits, or drug pickups.

Meal Delivery Programs

Some plans send meals to people who have been in the hospital or who are dealing with long-term health problems. Members of these programs usually get healthy, ready-made meals sent to their homes to help them get better or keep their health in check.

Telehealth Services

Telemedicine is being accepted by Medicare Advantage plans more and more, and they now cover virtual visits with doctors. This lets people talk to their doctors from home about non-emergency issues, managing a chronic illness, or getting follow-up care.

3. **Financial Protection and Out-of-Pocket Costs**

One big difference between Original Medicare and Medicare Advantage is that Medicare Advantage plans come with built-in financial protections:

Out-of-Pocket Maximums

Original Medicare doesn't limit out-of-pocket costs, but Medicare Advantage plans have to include a ceiling on how much you can spend each year. When this limit is reached, the plan pays for all of the beneficiary's medical bills for the rest of the year. This amount gives people a lot of financial security, especially those who have long-term illnesses or need to see a doctor often.

Cost Sharing

Medicare Advantage plans usually have copayments or coinsurance for things like visits to the doctor, talks with specialists, stays in the hospital, and prescription drugs. Plans vary in how much people pay for certain services, and some services may cost less with a Medicare Advantage plan than with Original Medicare. In some cases, though, other services might cost more, based on the plan.

4. **Coordination of Care**

Care coordination is something that Medicare Advantage plans often put a lot of stress on. In Health Maintenance Organization (HMO) plans, for example, members must pick a primary care physician (PCP) who will be in charge of their general care and refer them to specialists.

This model is meant to make sure that care is well-coordinated, which lowers the chance of treatments or breaks in care that aren't needed. Preferred Provider Organization (PPO) plans, on the other hand, give members more freedom by letting them see experts and doctors without referrals. However, out-of-network care usually costs more.

5. **Extra Services for Chronic Conditions**

Special Needs Plans (SNPs) are Medicare Advantage plans that are made for people with certain long-term diseases or other unique health needs. A lot of the time, these plans comes with extra benefits that are designed to help people with certain conditions. For example, people with diabetes or heart disease may be able to get help from professional case managers, educational programs that teach about their disease, or services that help them handle their medications. To sum up, Medicare Part C, also known as Medicare Advantage, provides several extra benefits.

How Part C Differs from Original Medicare

Original Medicare (Parts A and B) and Medicare Part C, also called Medicare Advantage, are different in several important ways, such as how the plans are set up, what they cover, and how costs are handled. **This is a full description of how Medicare Part C is different from Original Medicare:**

1. **Administration and Structure**

Original Medicare (Parts A and B)

Original Medicare is a federal health insurance program administered by the government, providing essential coverage to individuals who are 65 and older, as well as younger people with certain disabilities. **The program is divided into two key components:**

- **Part A (Hospital Insurance)**: This portion primarily covers inpatient hospital stays, care in a skilled nursing facility, hospice care, and some limited home health services. It helps beneficiaries cover the costs associated with hospital rooms, meals, and nursing services during their stay, as well as care following discharge when transitioning to a skilled nursing facility or receiving hospice care.
- **Part B (Medical Insurance)**: Part B focuses on outpatient services, providing coverage for doctor visits, preventive care, diagnostic tests, and medically necessary treatments. It also helps cover the cost of durable medical equipment (DME), such as wheelchairs, walkers, and other long-term medical aids needed for daily living. In addition to routine doctor visits, Part B includes preventive services like screenings for cancer, diabetes, and heart disease, along with vaccinations and wellness check-ups.

Together, Parts A and B offer a foundational level of coverage, though beneficiaries often seek supplemental plans to cover gaps not addressed by Original Medicare, such as prescription drugs or extended hospital stays. People who choose Original Medicare can go to any doctor or other healthcare provider that takes Medicare; they don't need a recommendation or have to stick to a network of providers.

Medicare Advantage (Part C): When you have Medicare Advantage (Part C), private insurance companies that are approved by Medicare handle Part C of Medicare. They are private insurers that offer plans that include both Part A and Part B of Medicare. These plans often include extra benefits that Original Medicare does not cover. You remain enrolled in Medicare but your benefits and claims are handled by private insurance instead of the federal government.

2. **Coverage Differences**

Original Medicare Coverage: The first version of Medicare covers hospital stays (Part A) and medical care (Part B), like doctor visits, outpatient care, and prevention care. **But Original Medicare doesn't cover a few important things:**

- Prescription drugs (unless the beneficiary enrolls in a separate Part D plan).
- Routine dental care.
- Vision care, including glasses or contact lenses.
- Hearing exams and hearing aids.
- Long-term care services (like custodial care in nursing homes).

Medicare Advantage Coverage: Medicare Advantage plans have to cover the same things that Original Medicare does, but many of them also give extra benefits. Some common extra benefits are:

- **Prescription drug coverage (Part D):** Most Medicare Advantage plans cover prescription drugs, so you don't need a separate Part D plan.
- **Vision, hearing, and dental care:** A lot of Medicare Advantage plans cover regular eye exams, teeth cleanings, hearing tests, and even glasses, contacts, or hearing aids.
- **Fitness and wellness programs:** Many plans offer exercise programs like SilverSneakers or health benefits like telehealth services and gym memberships.
- **Over-the-counter (OTC) benefits:** Some plans let you buy health goods like pills and medicines that aren't covered by your insurance.

3. **Provider Networks**

Original Medicare: The type of Medicare lets you see any doctor, expert, or hospital in the U.S. that takes Medicare. There are no network limits, so people who get Medicare can choose any doctor they want and don't need a referral to see an expert.

Medicare Advantage: Medicare Advantage plans usually have network limits that depend on the type of plan:

- **Health Maintenance Organization (HMO):** You can only see doctors in a certain network, and you usually need a referral to see a specialist. Most of the time, out-of-network care is not paid, but in some situations, it may be.
- **Preferred Provider Organization (PPO):** Gives you more choices by letting you see doctors who aren't in their network, but it costs more. Most of the time, referrals are not needed for specialists.
- **Private Fee-for-Service (PFFS):** This plan lets you see any doctor who agrees to the payment terms. However, treatments that aren't covered by the plan may cost more.

4. **Costs and Payments**

Original Medicare Costs

- **Part A (Hospital Insurance):** Most individuals do not have to pay a premium for Part A if they or their spouse have worked and contributed to Medicare taxes for at least 10 years (40 quarters). However, there are still out-of-pocket expenses. For hospital stays, beneficiaries are responsible for a deductible per benefit period, as well as coinsurance, if their hospital stay extends beyond a certain number of days. Skilled nursing facility care also has daily coinsurance costs after a specific number of covered days.

- **Part B (Medical Insurance)**: Part B requires a monthly premium, which is income-based, meaning higher-income individuals will pay more. Additionally, there is an annual deductible that must be met before Medicare covers most services. Once the deductible is satisfied, beneficiaries generally pay 20% of the Medicare-approved amount for most outpatient services, including doctor visits and medical procedures. One important aspect of Original Medicare is that it does not have a cap on out-of-pocket spending, leaving beneficiaries responsible for 20% of their medical bills with no limit on how much they may owe over time.

Medicare Advantage Costs

- **Monthly Premiums**: While most Medicare Advantage plans have low or even no additional monthly premiums, beneficiaries are still required to pay the standard Part B premium. Depending on the specific plan, there may be extra costs, such as a small premium for enhanced coverage or additional services.
- **Cost-Sharing Structure**: Unlike Original Medicare, Medicare Advantage plans often replace the 20% coinsurance model with set copayments or coinsurance amounts for doctor visits, hospital stays, and other services. This means that, instead of paying a percentage of the total cost, beneficiaries pay a fixed dollar amount for covered services, providing more predictability in their healthcare expenses.
- **Annual Out-of-Pocket Maximum**: One significant advantage of Medicare Advantage plans is the inclusion of an annual out-of-pocket maximum. This means that once a beneficiary reaches a certain spending threshold for covered services, the plan covers 100% of the remaining healthcare costs for the rest of the year. This cap offers financial protection against high medical expenses, which is not available in Original Medicare.

5. **Supplemental Coverage**

Original Medicare: A lot of people who choose this plan also buy Medigap (Medicare Supplement Insurance) to help pay for costs like copayments, deductibles, and coinsurance. Private companies sell Medigap policies, which work with Original Medicare to cover bills that Medicare doesn't pay. Advantage plans for Medicare do not work with Medigap.

Medicare Advantage: Medigap plans can't be used with Medicare Advantage plans. There are, however, times when Medicare Advantage plans with lower yearly and out-of-pocket costs mean that some people don't need extra benefits. Some people may not need to have more than one insurance policy because their Medicare Advantage plan covers things like dental, eye, and hearing care.

6. **Enrollment and Switching**

Original Medicare: It's easy to sign up for Original Medicare. When most people turn 65 and are already getting Social Security benefits, they are automatically signed up for Parts A and B. You can change your Medicare plan to a Medicare Advantage plan or add a Part D prescription drug plan at certain times of the year.

Medicare Advantage: There are certain times when you can sign up for Medicare Advantage plans:

- o **Initial Enrollment Period (IEP):** The seven-month period surrounding your 65th birthday when you can sign up for Medicare Advantage.
- o **Annual Enrollment Period (AEP):** The Annual Enrollment Period (AEP) is every year from October 15 to December 7. This is when you can change Medicare Advantage plans or switch from Original Medicare to Medicare Advantage.
- o **Medicare Advantage Open Enrollment Period (OEP):** The Medicare Advantage Open Enrollment Period (OEP) occurs from January 1 to March 31 each year. During this time, individuals already enrolled in a Medicare Advantage plan have the option to switch to another Medicare Advantage plan or return to Original Medicare.

7. **Out-of-Country Coverage**

Original Medicare: Most of the time, healthcare services gotten outside of the U.S. are not covered by Original Medicare. Some Medigap plans may cover limited foreign travel emergencies.

Medicare Advantage: Most Medicare Advantage plans don't cover a lot of medical care outside of the U.S., but some may cover emergency or urgent care while you're away. It's important to look at what each plan says about foreign care and what it doesn't cover.

The pros and cons of Medicare Advantage plans

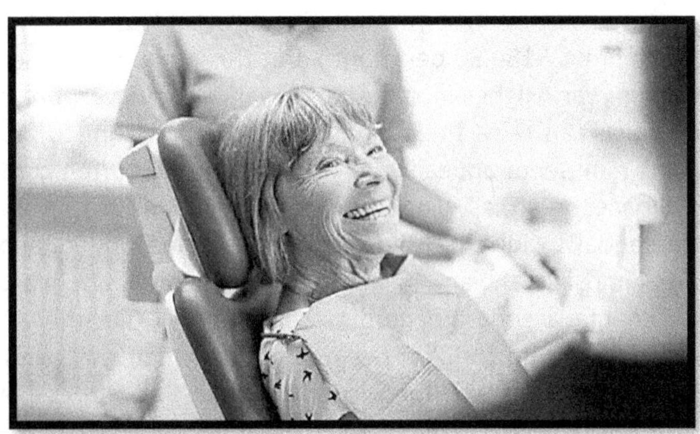

When you choose your Medicare plan every year, the most important thing to think about is whether to go with Original Medicare or a Medicare Advantage plan (also called Medicare Part C) from a private health provider. There isn't a one-size-fits-all solution. However, Medicare Advantage plans, such as those promoted in TV commercials with well-known personalities, come with their own advantages and disadvantages that should be carefully considered before enrolling. Part C plans are very different from Original Medicare, which is also known as "fee-for-service": Many Medicare Advantage plans only cover a small group of doctors and hospitals. If you can see a provider who isn't in their network, it will cost you more.

In 2024, Medicare Open Enrollment runs from October 15 to December 7. This means that you need to decide quickly whether to switch to Medicare Advantage or Original Medicare. You can switch Medicare Advantage plans or go back to Original Medicare if you'd rather from January to March 2024. More Medicare beneficiaries are opting for Medicare Advantage plans, primarily because they believe these plans offer more benefits and lower healthcare costs compared to Original Medicare. This year, for the first time, half of all Medicare beneficiaries are expected to be enrolled in Medicare Advantage plans, up from just 37% in 2018. According to a report by KFF, the average Medicare beneficiary has 43 Medicare Advantage plans to choose from, with nearly 4,000 options nationwide. To enroll in a Medicare Advantage plan, you must first sign up for Original Medicare Part A (hospital insurance) and Part B (medical insurance). Most Medicare Advantage plans include prescription drug coverage through Part D. However, if you choose Medicare Advantage, you cannot also have a separate Medigap insurance policy, which is an option available with Original Medicare. Several major insurance companies, including Aetna, Blue Cross Blue Shield, Cigna, Humana, Kaiser Permanente, and UnitedHealthcare, offer Medicare Part C (Medicare Advantage) plans. **Below is a breakdown of the advantages and disadvantages of Medicare Advantage plans.**

Pros of Medicare Advantage plans

1. **Potentially lower out-of-pocket costs than Original Medicare**

Some Medicare Advantage plans offer the enticing benefit of no monthly premiums and, in some cases, even help cover part or all of your Medicare Part B premium. For instance, in 2023, the standard Part B premium is $164.90 per month, but this amount is projected to increase by around 3% in the coming year. Higher-income beneficiaries, however, are required to pay an additional surcharge, which can raise their monthly Part B premium to as much as $560.50. While $0 premium plans may seem appealing at first glance, they often come with higher out-of-pocket costs for services such as diagnostic tests, hospital stays, specialist visits, and outpatient care. It's essential to look beyond the premium and understand the full scope of potential costs before choosing a plan. In addition to $0 premium plans, some Medicare Advantage plans may charge a separate monthly premium. While the average premium is around $18, some plans charge up to $200 per month for enhanced coverage and additional benefits. Medicare Advantage plans also tend to offer lower, flat-rate co-pays for services like doctor visits, in contrast to the 20% coinsurance required by Original Medicare for Part B services. However, out-of-network providers may come with higher co-pays or coinsurance costs. A key benefit of Medicare Advantage plans is that they include an annual out-of-pocket limit for Medicare-covered services under Parts A and B. This provides a cap on how much beneficiaries will need to pay in a given year, which is not available in Original Medicare. For 2023, the out-of-pocket maximum for in-network services is set at $8,300, while for out-of-network services; it can reach up to $12,450. Although some Medicare Advantage plans do not have an annual deductible, others require beneficiaries to meet deductibles for Part B and Part D services, according to the National Council on Aging. The presence or absence of a deductible can vary based on the specific plan.

2. **Additional Benefits Beyond Original Medicare**

Medicare Advantage plans are required to provide coverage for all the services covered by Original Medicare, but they often come with additional benefits. Some of the most common extras include coverage for dental, vision, and hearing services. However, these added benefits often come with certain limitations. For example, dental coverage may only include one cleaning per year, or benefits might be capped at $1,000 annually. Vision care typically has limits as well, with some plans capping benefits at $160 per year for eyeglasses or contact lenses. In addition to healthcare-related benefits, many Medicare Advantage plans offer other perks such as pre-paid cards for purchasing over-the-counter medications, health supplies, or bathroom safety equipment. Some plans may also offer caregiver support services. Non-medical benefits can include things like free gym memberships, meal delivery services, transportation to the grocery store or bank, and programs aimed at reducing social isolation for older adults.

3. **No Denials Based on Pre-Existing Conditions**

Medicare Advantage plans are required by law to accept all individuals who are eligible for Medicare, regardless of their health status or pre-existing conditions. This guarantees that beneficiaries will not be denied coverage based on their medical history.

4. **coordinated Care and Higher Satisfaction Levels**

Research indicates that Medicare Advantage enrollees often experience more coordinated care compared to those in Original Medicare. According to two studies from the Commonwealth Fund, Medicare Advantage beneficiaries were more likely to have access to comprehensive care management, including consistent healthcare providers, treatment plans, and regular medication reviews. Additionally, Medicare Advantage enrollees reported better access to healthcare services between appointments. Satisfaction rates are high across both Medicare Advantage and Original Medicare, with more than 90% of enrollees expressing satisfaction with the quality of care. While both programs generally report similar satisfaction levels, Medicare Advantage is known for offering better access to preventive care services such as annual wellness visits, routine screenings, and vaccinations. A 2022 review of 62 studies found that Medicare Advantage outperformed traditional Medicare in areas such as preventive services and had lower rates of hospital readmissions. For beneficiaries with chronic conditions like diabetes, Medicare Advantage members were more likely to receive care in line with clinical guidelines, such as regular diabetic eye exams. However, both Medicare Advantage and Original Medicare showed similar outcomes in managing conditions like blood sugar levels.

Cons of Medicare Advantage plans

Limited doctor and hospital networks: The Medicare Advantage plan you choose will significantly impact the type of care you receive and the associated costs. Each plan comes with its own network of doctors, hospitals, and other healthcare providers. These networks are subject to change annually, so it's important to review your plan's provider options regularly. One potential challenge with Medicare Advantage plans is finding specialized care, such as therapy services. A study published by *Health Affairs* revealed that nearly half of the counties examined lacked therapists who participate in Medicare Advantage networks. This can create barriers to accessing mental health services, particularly in rural areas or regions with fewer providers. If you relocate or maintain a second home in another part of the country, it can also complicate your care. Depending on your Medicare Advantage plan, visits to doctors outside your plan's network may result in higher out-of-pocket costs. It's critical to verify if your plan allows out-of-network visits and, if so, whether you can find a doctor willing to accept the plan's terms.

Common Types of Medicare Advantage Plans

The two most common types of Medicare Advantage plans are Health Maintenance Organizations (HMOs) and Preferred Provider Organizations (PPOs).

- **Health Maintenance Organization (HMO)**: HMOs generally require you to use healthcare providers within their network for most services. If you need to see a specialist, you will usually need a referral and prior authorization. While this type of plan tends to have lower premiums and out-of-pocket costs, it limits your flexibility in choosing doctors or specialists outside of the network.
- **Preferred Provider Organization (PPO)**: PPOs offer more flexibility, allowing beneficiaries to visit out-of-network providers, but at a higher cost compared to in-network visits. Unlike HMOs, PPOs typically do not require referrals for specialist appointments. However, the trade-off is that PPOs often come with higher premiums and cost-sharing limits, so you may pay more overall for the increased provider flexibility.

Prior Authorization Challenges

Many Medicare Advantage plans require prior authorization for certain services or treatments. While intended to manage healthcare costs and ensure appropriate care, this process can sometimes delay or even deny necessary care. In 2021 alone, nearly 2 million prior authorization requests from Medicare Advantage beneficiaries were denied, according to a report by KFF, a nonpartisan organization that tracks healthcare issues. The Health and Human Services Inspector General has also flagged this as a systemic issue. To address these concerns, the Biden administration introduced new rules for prior authorization, which are set to take effect in 2024. These rules aim to make the process more transparent and streamlined, reducing the likelihood of inappropriate care denials. Some states and insurers are also making changes, such as eliminating prior authorization requirements for highly regarded doctors and hospitals, to improve access to timely care.

Wait Times for Care

A study by the *Commonwealth Fund* found that beneficiaries of both Medicare Advantage and Traditional Medicare experience similar wait times for care. On average, patients wait over a month for doctor's appointments and about three weeks for outpatient hospital services. This suggests that while Medicare Advantage plans may offer more coordinated care, they do not necessarily guarantee faster access to providers compared to Traditional Medicare.

Access to High-Quality Care

According to a 2022 KFF report, Traditional Medicare outperformed Medicare Advantage in providing access to top-tier hospitals, skilled nursing facilities, and home health agencies. This was particularly noticeable for beneficiaries needing specialized care, such as cancer treatments. Therefore, individuals who prioritize access to high-quality providers may find Traditional Medicare a better fit, though it often requires additional coverage like a Medigap policy to fill in gaps.

Employer or Union Health Coverage Considerations

If you are covered by an employer or union health plan, enrolling in a Medicare Advantage plan may cause you to lose this coverage. In many cases, the loss of employer or union-sponsored coverage extends to family members, such as a spouse or dependents. It is crucial to review the details of your employer's health benefits before making a switch, to ensure you don't forfeit important coverage for yourself or your family. Additionally, once employer or union coverage is lost, it may not be possible to reinstate it.

Challenges with Switching Medicare Plans

Switching between Medicare plans can present challenges, particularly when moving between Traditional Medicare and Medicare Advantage. If you switch from Traditional Medicare to Medicare Advantage, you lose access to Medigap policies, which help cover out-of-pocket costs under Original Medicare. Conversely, if you switch back from Medicare Advantage to Traditional Medicare, you may face difficulties purchasing a Medigap policy due to pre-existing health conditions. This can leave you exposed to higher out-of-pocket costs in Traditional Medicare.

How to Learn More about Medicare Advantage

For individuals looking to explore Medicare Advantage plans in more detail, Medicare.gov provides a range of resources. The Medicare Plan Finder tool allows users to compare plans based on coverage, costs, and customer satisfaction. Star ratings for service quality are also available. You can also contact the State Health Insurance Assistance Programs (SHIPs), which offer free counseling and assistance with Medicare questions. These experts can help guide you through the decision-making process based on your specific healthcare needs. If you prefer to work with a professional advisor, it's advisable to seek recommendations from trusted sources, such as your doctor or friends. The National Council on Aging's Medicare Standards of

Excellence list is another reliable resource for finding qualified advisors who put your interests first.

Types of Medicare Advantage Plans

Medicare Advantage (Part C) gives people different types of plans to choose from based on their specific health care needs. All Medicare Advantage plans must cover at least the same things as Original Medicare (Parts A and B), but they often offer extra benefits like covering prescription drugs, eye, dental, and hearing needs. Private insurance companies that work with Medicare run these plans. Each one is different in how it handles healthcare, the doctors it covers, and the prices. **Here is a more in-depth look at the main kinds of Medicare Advantage plans that people can get:**

1. **Health Maintenance Organization (HMO) Plans**

Overview: Health Maintenance Organization (HMO) plans are one type of Medicare Advantage plan that you may see. Their main business is offering health care through a network of contracted health care providers, such as hospitals, doctors, and experts. People who are covered by the plan must go to these network providers, unless they need urgent or emergency care.

Key Features:
- **Network Restrictions:** One of the most important things about an HMO plan is that patients must choose healthcare doctors and places that are in the plan's network. Services you get outside of the network usually won't be covered, unless it's an emergency or you need quick care while you're moving.
- **Primary Care Physician (PCP) Requirement:** Most HMO plans make members choose a primary care physician (PCP). The PCP is the person who handles the person's care and is the first person they talk to about their health needs. To see a specialist or get other advanced medical care, you usually need a referral from your primary care doctor.
- **Lower Costs:** Most of the time, HMO plans have lower rates and out-of-pocket costs than other Medicare Advantage plans. This is because they focus on in-network care and organized care through a PCP. This makes HMO plans a good choice for people who want to keep their healthcare costs low and don't mind having a limited number of providers to choose from.

Pros and Cons:
- **Pros:** Lower premiums and out-of-pocket costs, care coordination through a primary care physician (PCP), and a focus on preventive care.
- **Cons:** You can't choose from many providers, you need a referral to see a specialist, and you aren't covered for out-of-network care (except in emergencies).

Who It's Best For: HMO plans are great for people who don't mind having to be referred to a specialist for care and don't mind getting care from a set network of providers. They're good for people who want more control over their healthcare and lower out-of-pocket costs.

2. **Preferred Provider Organization (PPO) Plans**

Overview: Another popular type of Medicare Advantage plan that gives you more freedom than HMO plans is the Preferred Provider Organization (PPO) plan. PPO plans also have a network of doctors and hospitals they work with, but users can also go to doctors and hospitals that are not in their network, though it will cost them more.

Key Features:
- **Flexibility in Choosing Providers:** People who have PPO plans can see any doctor, even ones who aren't in the plan's network, without getting a referral. However, it usually costs less to use in-network companies because they have worked out deals with the plan to lower their prices.
- **No Requirement for Referrals:** Unlike HMO plans, PPO plans don't make members choose a main care doctor or get referrals to see specialists. This freedom can be especially appealing to recipients who would rather get specialized care more quickly.
- **Cost Structure:** When it comes to prices, PPO plans tend to have higher deductibles and fees than HMO plans. This is especially true for people who see a lot of doctors who are not in their network. On the other hand, a lot of users are ready to pay these higher prices so they can get care from providers outside the network.
- **Out-of-Pocket Limits:** All Medicare Advantage plans, including PPO plans, have a maximum amount of money that you can spend each year. When this limit is met, the plan pays for all covered medical costs for the rest of the year.

Pros and Cons:
- **Pros:** You can choose from a wider range of healthcare providers, you don't need a recommendation, and you can get coverage for out-of-network care (though it will cost you more).
- **Cons:** Compared to HMO plans, they have higher premiums and out-of-pocket costs, especially for services that are not covered by the plan.

Who It's Best For: People who value freedom in their healthcare decisions and are ready to pay more to see doctors outside of their network should consider PPO plans. People who want to take charge of their care and don't need recommendations or a primary care doctor will like this plan.

3. Private Fee-for-Service (PFFS) Plans

Overview: There is an option for HMOs and PPOs called Private Fee-for-Service (PFFS) plans. These plans let plan members see any doctor who agrees to the plan's payment terms and conditions. There are no provider networks that PFFS plans have to follow, but some plans may have a network of companies that have decided to follow the plan's rules.

Key Features:
- **Provider Flexibility:** Because there are no specific network limits, PFFS plans to give plan participants a lot of freedom in picking healthcare providers. It's important to remember, though, that service companies must agree to the plan's terms and rates for payment. In other words, a provider may agree to take Medicare but not a certain Medicare PFFS plan.

- o **No Need for Referrals:** Just like PPO plans, PFFS plans don't require their members to get referrals to see specialists or get certain services. Beneficiaries can go to any provider who is willing to work with the plan's payment terms.
  - o **Cost Variability:** PFFS plans can let you choose your provider, but the prices for services can change a lot based on whether the provider agrees to the rules of the plan. You may also have to pay more for services that aren't covered by your HMO or PPO plan than for services that are.
  - o **Optional Network:** Some PFFS plans may have a network of providers who have decided to follow the plan's rules. Beneficiaries may pay less when they use in-network providers than when they go out-of-network providers.

Pros and Cons:
  - o **Pros:** You can choose which providers to use, you don't need referrals, and there are no limits on the network.
  - o **Cons:** Providers may not agree to the plan's rules, which could limit your access to providers and cause your out-of-pocket costs to go up.

Who It's Best For: PFFS plans work best for people who like having options and don't mind finding out ahead of time if the companies they choose will accept the plan. People who travel a lot or live in rural places where provider networks may be weak should consider this choice.

4. **Special Needs Plans (SNPs)**

Overview: Special Needs Plans, or SNPs, are a type of Medicare Advantage plan that is meant to meet the unique health care needs of people with certain conditions. People who have certain long-term diseases, who are qualified for both Medicare and Medicaid or who live in institutions like nursing homes can use these plans.

Types of SNPs:

Special Needs Plans come in three different types:
  - o **Chronic Condition SNP (C-SNP):** This type of SNP is made for people who have serious or disabling chronic conditions like diabetes, heart disease, or lung problems that don't go away. These plans offer specialized care and services that are designed to help people with certain health conditions.
  - o **Dual Eligible SNP (D-SNP):** There is a plan called Dual qualified SNP (D-SNP) that helps people who are qualified for both Medicare and Medicaid. D-SNPs help Medicare and Medicaid work together better, which means that patients often pay less out of pocket and can get Medicaid-covered services that regular Medicare Advantage plans might not cover.
  - o **Institutional SNP (I-SNP):** These plans are made for people who live in long-term care homes or need care at the institutional level. I-SNPs focus on giving this group of people the specialty medical care they need, such as managing chronic illnesses and coordinating care.

Key Features:
  - o **Tailored Care:** SNPs are very specialized and make sure that the care they give meets the needs of the people they serve. A C-SNP for diabetes might include things like

diabetes education, specialized medical tools, and care management to keep blood sugar levels in check.
- o **Network Requirements:** Like HMO plans, SNPs generally have network limits, which means people who sign up for them can only get care from the plan's network of providers, unless it's an emergency.
- o **Care Coordination:** SNPs put a lot of stress on care coordination and often give beneficiaries access to case managers or care coordinators who help ensure their healthcare needs are met.

Pros and Cons:
- o **Pros:** Specialized care for people with unique health needs, benefits that are tailored to each person, and care management.
- o **Cons:** It's only available to people who meet certain requirements, like having a chronic disease, being eligible for dual coverage, or being in an institution for care. There are also network limits.

Who It's Best For: People with difficult or long-term health problems that need specialized care, people who are eligible for both Medicare and Medicaid or people who live in long-term care facilities are the best candidates for SNPs. People who need organized, all-around health care services will love these plans.

5. **Medicare Medical Savings Account (MSA) Plans**

Overview: A Medicare Medical Savings Account (MSA) plan is a type of Medicare Advantage plan that is not very popular. It mixes a high-deductible health plan with a medical savings account. The savings account gets money from the plan that can be used to pay for medical costs before the high deductible is met.

Key Features:
- o **High-Deductible Health Plan:** MSA plans come with a high-deductible health plan that doesn't pay for services until the beneficiary meets the deductible. Most of the time, the plan's cost is higher than those of other Medicare Advantage plans.
- o **Medical Savings Account:** Some MSA plans also come with a savings account that Medicare puts money into annually. Beneficiaries can use this money to pay for medical costs that are allowed by law, even if Medicare doesn't cover them. After the fee is met, the plan will pay for covered services.
- o **Flexibility in Provider Choice:** You can choose which providers to work with, just like with PFFS plans. MSA plans don't usually have a network of providers. Medicare recipients can see any doctor or hospital that takes Medicare; this gives them more choices when it comes to their health care.

Pros and Cons:
- o **Pros:** Flexibility in choosing providers, ability to use savings account funds for medical expenses, no network restrictions.
- o **Cons:** There is a high deductible before the plan benefits start to kick in, and you have to be careful with your savings account to pay for medical costs.

Who It's Best For: MSA plans work best for people who are generally healthy and don't expect to have many medical bills. People who want to be in charge of how their healthcare dollars are spent and are used to handling a high-deductible plan will like these plans.

6.   **HMO Point-of-Service (HMO-POS) Plans**

Health Maintenance Organization (HMO) plans come in different forms, one of which is HMO Point-of-Service (HMO-POS) plans. They have some of the structure and benefits of an HMO plan along with some of the flexibility that you'd find in a Preferred Provider Organization (PPO) plan. These plans still work mostly within a set network of healthcare providers, but they do let users get some services from outside the network, though it generally costs more. People who like the lower costs of an HMO but want the freedom to go to a doctor outside the network when they need to may be interested in HMO-POS plans.

Key Features:

- **In-Network and Out-of-Network Services:** Just like with a traditional HMO plan, you'll save the most money if you use doctors and hospitals in the plan's network for most services. You can go out-of-network for some services, though it generally costs more with these plans. This gives you more freedom than with a standard HMO.
- **Referrals for Specialists:** Even if you want to see a specialist in the same network, most HMO-POS plans still make you pick a primary care provider (PCP) and get a referral from that PCP. This method helps organize care and makes sure that your PCP knows about all of your treatments.
- **Higher Costs for Out-of-Network Services:** You can choose to go out of network with an HMO or POS plan, but the cost-sharing amounts (like copayments or coinsurance) are generally higher than for services that are in your network. Sometimes, the plan may only pay a portion of the cost for services that are not in their network. The client will have to pay the rest.
- **Out-of-Pocket Maximums:** There is an annual out-of-pocket maximum for HMO-POS plans, just like there is one for other Medicare Advantage plans. This is the most you'll have to pay for approved treatments in a year. Once you hit this amount, the plan will cover all of your costs for approved services for the rest of the year, no matter if they are in-network or not. However, out-of-network costs usually contribute less toward the out-of-pocket maximum.

Flexibility in Care

One of the best things about an HMO-POS plan is that it strikes a good mix between an HMO's low cost and a PPO's flexibility. If you have a regular HMO, you would not pay for care that is not in the network (except in some situations). People with HMO-POS plans can get care from doctors who are not in their network, but it's important to think about the higher costs that come with that. For instance, you might want to see an expert who is not in your insurance plan, but has a history of working with your family. Under a regular HMO, that out-of-network specialist would not be covered. However, under an HMO-POS plan, some of the costs would be covered, but at a higher rate than for in-network specialists.

Cost Structure:

- o **In-Network Costs:** When you use in-network providers, HMO-POS plans usually have low copayments or coinsurance amounts, just like standard HMOs. The total cost of care is usually less than with PPO plans, which includes fees and out-of-pocket costs.
- o **Out-of-Network Costs:** Eligible People can choose to get some services from providers outside of their network, but the costs are typically higher. This could mean paying more for copayments, coinsurance, or even the full cost of some services if your plan only covers some out-of-network care.

Prescription Drug Coverage: There are a lot of HMO-POS plans that also include Medicare Part D (prescription drug coverage). There is no longer a need to sign up for a different Medicare Part D plan. But, based on the plan's formulary and network deals, medication services that aren't in the plan's network may also cost more.

Pros and Cons:

Pros:

- o **Greater Flexibility:** This makes it possible to get some services from outside the network, which isn't usually possible with a traditional HMO.
- o **Lower In-Network Costs:** In-network services cost less with a PPO plan, just like they do with an HMO.
- o **Care Coordination:** Primary care doctors (PCPs) help oversee all of a patient's care, making sure that all services and treatments work together and that patients don't have to go through needless tests or treatments more than once.

Cons:

- o **Higher Out-of-Network Costs:** You can get care from someone outside the network, but for most services, the prices are higher.
- o **Referrals Required:** Just like in a regular HMO, you still need a request from your primary care doctor (PCP) to see a specialist, even if the specialist is in your network. This can be a problem for some people.
- o **Limited Coverage for Out-of-Network Services:** Some HMO-POS plans may not cover all out-of-network services or may only cover a part of the prices.

Who It's Best For:

- o **Balance Seekers:** HMO-POS plans are great for people who want the freedom of a PPO plan and the cost savings of a traditional HMO plan. This kind of plan is great for people who want to be able to see doctors who are not in their network when they need to but would rather use in-network services most of the time.
- o **Individuals Who Want Cost Control:** An HMO-POS plan has lower rates and in-network costs, which is great for people who want lower out-of-pocket costs and don't mind working with a PCP for recommendations.
- o **People Who Travel Frequently:** Being able to go out-of-network and still have some service can be very helpful if you travel a lot or live in a different area for part of the year and your plan's network may not be as strong there.

Medicare Part D (Prescription Drug Coverage)

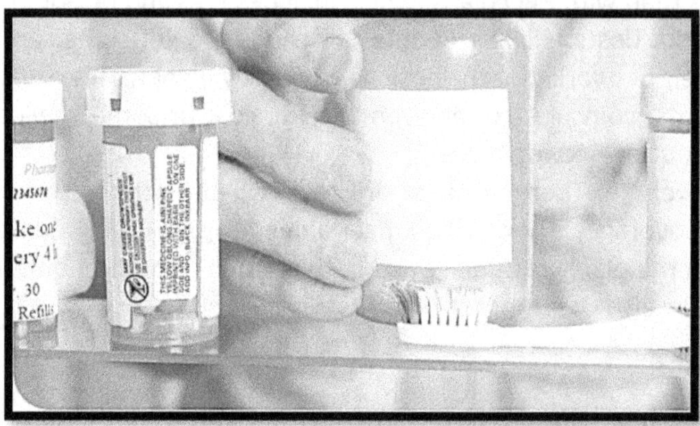

Part D of Medicare covers prescription drugs. Anyone eligible for Medicare can choose to get this benefit. It can be added to Original Medicare (Parts A and B) or some Medicare Advantage (Part C) plans that cover prescription drugs. Part D is very important for helping Medicare recipients pay for their medications because Original Medicare doesn't cover most outpatient prescription drugs.

How Medicare Part D Works

Part D of Medicare is offered by private insurance companies that are approved by Medicare. There are different plans from these companies, and each one has its list of drugs that are covered (formulary), copayments or coinsurance amounts, and fees. People who are eligible for Medicare can sign up for either a separate Medicare Part D Prescription Drug Plan (PDP) or a Medicare Advantage plan that covers drugs (called a Medicare Advantage Prescription Drug plan or MAPD).

Standalone Part D Plans (PDPs)

These plans are made to cover prescription drugs on top of Original Medicare (Parts A and B), some Medicare Cost Plans, and Medicare Medical Savings Account (MSA) plans. People with Original Medicare often buy a Part D plan to cover the cost of their medical medicines.

Medicare Advantage Prescription Drug Plans (MAPDs)

Prescription drugs are covered by a lot of Medicare Advantage plans. These plans offer Medicare users a more complete package by combining all their benefits into one plan, including hospital, medical, and prescription drug coverage.

Coverage and Formularies

The formulary for each Medicare Part D plan is a list of the drugs that the plan will pay for. The list is broken up into tiers, and each tier determines the amount of cost-sharing used:
- **Tier 1:** Usually includes generic drugs, which are the cheapest.
- **Tier 2:** Usually has the most popular brand-name drugs.
- **Tier 3:** Covers non-preferred brand-name drugs, which are more expensive.
- **Specialty Tier:** Includes very high-cost drugs, often for rare or complex conditions.

Since plans' formularies can change from year to year, users need to check their plan's list of drugs that are covered during the Annual Enrollment Period (AEP). If a beneficiary needs a medicine that isn't covered, they can ask for an exception or switch to a different plan.

Costs in Medicare Part D

Part D of Medicare has different costs based on the plan, the drugs a person takes, and the pharmacy they go to. Below is a list of the usual costs:

Monthly Premiums

Part D Medicare plans have a monthly premium that can be very different depending on the plan and its benefits. You may pay this fee along with other plan costs if you get prescription drug coverage through a Medicare Advantage plan.

Annual Deductible

A lot of Medicare Part D plans have a deductible every year. The highest payment that Medicare will cover for Part D plans in 2024 is $545. Some plans may have smaller or no deductibles, but the fees are usually higher because of this.

Copayments and Coinsurance

After the deductible is met, beneficiaries usually pay a copayment, which is a set amount, or coinsurance, which is a portion of the drug's cost, for each prescription. This depends on the tier of the drug. Generic drugs and other lower-tier drugs usually have lower copayments, while specialty drugs and higher-tier drugs have higher cost-sharing requirements.

Coverage Gap (Donut Hole)

There is a coverage gap in Medicare Part D, which is sometimes called the **donut hole.** Once a beneficiary and their plan spend a certain amount on covered medicines, they enter the donut hole and may have to pay a higher portion of drug costs. In 2024, this threshold is $5,030. During the donut hole, beneficiaries pay **25% of the cost** of both generic and brand-name drugs. Healthcare changes have slowly stopped the donut hole, but people who are benefiting from them may still have higher out-of-pocket costs during this time. When beneficiaries hit a certain out-of-pocket limit, they move into catastrophic coverage.

Catastrophic Coverage

A person will be eligible for catastrophic coverage once their total out-of-pocket drug costs, including those paid during the coverage gap, hit the catastrophic coverage ($8,000 in 2024). During this time, the beneficiary only has to pay a small copayment or coinsurance for drugs that are covered for the rest of the year. Medicare pays for most of the cost.

Late Enrollment Penalty

Medicare beneficiaries should sign up for a Part D plan as soon as they become qualified unless they already have drug coverage that is at least as good as Medicare's. They might have to pay a late enrollment charge if they don't sign up when they are first qualified and don't have coverage that counts. This penalty is a constant rise in the monthly payment that is based on how long the beneficiary did not have insurance. Each month that you don't have creditable coverage costs you an extra 1% of your national base recipient payment. This amount is added to your premium forever. Like, if a person didn't have coverage for a year, their rate would go up by 12% of the national base premium for as long as they have Part D.

Medicare Part D Extra Help (Low-Income Subsidy Program)

The Extra Help program, which is also called the Low-Income Subsidy (LIS), can help people who are eligible but don't have a lot of money or resources pay for Part D. Extra Help lowers or gets rid of prescription drug fees, deductibles, and copayments. Beneficiaries must meet certain limits on their income and assets to be eligible. People whose income is up to 150% of the government poverty level may be able to get full or partial Extra Help in 2024. Extra Help is a big benefit for people who have trouble paying for their medicines because they are very expensive. It makes sure that people with low incomes can get the meds they need.

Medicare Part D and Employer Coverage

Some people who get Medicare keep working or get coverage through a spouse's workplace after they get Medicare. They don't have to sign up for a Part D plan right away if they have prescription drug coverage through their job, as long as the workplace plan is considered creditable coverage. If your drug coverage is at least as good as Medicare Part D, that's called **creditable coverage.** Beneficiaries should get a letter from their workplace saying if their prescription drug coverage is creditable. They have a **Special Enrollment Period** (SEP) to sign up for Part D without having to pay a late registration fee if they lose this coverage.

Annual Enrollment and Plan Changes

Every year, Medicare Part D plans can change their copays, formularies, and how members pay for things. These changes mean that people with Medicare can look at and change their Part D plan every year during the Medicare Annual Enrollment Period (AEP), which lasts from October 15 to December 7. **During this time, beneficiaries can:**
- Switch from one Part D plan to another.
- Drop Part D coverage if they no longer want or need it.
- Switch from Original Medicare with a separate Part D plan to a Medicare Advantage plan with prescription drug coverage (MAPD), or vice versa.

Beneficiaries must check their plan's formulary and cost structure every year to make sure it still meets their needs. This is especially important if they have been given new medicines or if something has changed with their health.

Part D Plan Tiers and Formularies

There is a list of drugs that are covered by each Part D plan called a formulary. These drugs are grouped into different price levels or tiers. In general:
- **Tier 1:** Typically, generic drugs have the lowest cost.
- **Tier 2:** Preferred brand-name drugs, more expensive than Tier 1, but still reasonably priced.
- **Tier 3:** Non-preferred brand-name drugs, which cost more.
- **Tier 4:** Specialty drugs, which are the most expensive medications, are often used for serious or chronic conditions.

Plans can change their formularies at any time during the year, but they have to let users know about any changes that could affect their medicines. Beneficiaries can ask for an exception if the drug they need is not on the formulary or is moved up in the tiers.

Formulary Tiers and Costs

Formulary tiers are a way for Medicare Part D plans to group prescription drugs and figure out how much they cost. There are usually both generic and brand-name drugs on the schedule, which is a list of the medicines that the plan offers. There are different levels of cost-sharing in the list, which is broken up into **tiers**. Most of the time, drugs in lower tiers have cheaper copayments or coinsurance. Drugs in higher tiers and above cost more. It's important to understand how the tier system works and how much each tier costs.

What Is a Formulary?

It is a list of the prescription drugs that a Medicare Part D plan or a Medicare Advantage Prescription Drug (MAPD) plan will pay for. Formularies are usually set up in tiers, and each plan makes its own. Plans' formularies can be different, so users need to check their plan's formulary to ensure that the medicines they take are covered. If a beneficiary needs a drug that isn't on the list, they can ask for an exception or think about moving to a different plan. Part D plans must cover at least two drugs from each treatment group or class, and they must cover all or most of the drugs in certain protected classes, such as

- Antidepressants
- Antipsychotics
- Anticonvulsants
- Immunosuppressants
- Cancer medications

Understanding Formulary Tiers

A **tiered system** is used by most Medicare Part D plans to group drugs on their formulary. Every tier has a different cost amount. For beneficiaries, drugs in lower tiers cost less, while drugs in higher tiers cost more. Most of the time, the tier system looks like this:

Tier 1: Generic Drugs

- **What It Includes:** Usually, this level covers **generic drugs**, which are medicines that have the same active ingredients as brand-name drugs but are a lot less expensive.
- **Cost:** For Tier 1 drugs, beneficiaries pay the least amount of copayment or coinsurance. With some plans, the cost is as low as $0 and as high as a small copayment of $1 to $10 per medication.
- **Who it's best For:** The lower out-of-pocket costs in this tier will help people who take popular, low-cost medicines.

Tier 2: Preferred Brand-Name Drugs

- **What It Includes: Preferred brand-name drugs** are usually in Tier 2. These are brand-name drugs that the insurance company has arranged lower prices for, making them more affordable than brand-name drugs that aren't as popular.

- **Cost:** Drugs in Tier 2 cost more than generics in Tier 1, but they are still cheaper than drugs in higher tiers. Different plans may have copayments for Tier 2 drugs that run from $20 to $40 or more.
- **Who it's best For:** People whose plans prefer brand-name drugs will save money with this tier.

Tier 3: Non-Preferred Brand-Name Drugs

- **What It Includes:** Tier 3 usually includes **non-preferred brand-name drugs**. These are brand-name drugs that the insurance plan thinks are less cost-effective or aren't given as often, so you'll have to pay more for them.
- **Cost:** Tier 3 drugs often have copayments or coinsurance that is much higher than Tier 2 drugs. Each order can cost $40 to $100 or more. In many plans, people who get Tier 3 drugs have to pay a bigger share of the cost of the drug as coinsurance.
- **Who it's best For:** People who need certain brand-name drugs that the plan doesn't cover will have to pay more, but they might not have any other choice if a generic or chosen drug isn't available.

Tier 4: Specialty Drugs

- **What It Includes:** Tier 4 is only for **specialty drugs**, which are expensive medicines used to treat unique or complicated illnesses like cancer, rheumatoid arthritis, or multiple sclerosis. Often, these drugs need to be handled, given, or watched in a certain way.
- **Cost:** When it comes to cost, specialty drugs are usually the most expensive. Instead of a flat copayment, beneficiaries usually have to pay coinsurance, which is a portion of the drug's cost. Coinsurance rates can be as high as 25% to 33% or more, which means the recipient may have to pay a lot of money for their medical care, especially for very expensive specialty drugs.
- **Who It's Best For:** Tier 4 drugs can help people with dangerous, long-lasting, or uncommon conditions who need specialized care. But, because these medicines are so expensive, it's important to plan for them and look into help programs if you need to.

Costs in Each Tier

Different plans have different drug prices, but here is a rough idea of what you can expect to pay depending on the tier:

Tier	Drug Type	Copayment/Coinsurance
Tier 1	Generic drugs	$0 - $10 (usually low copayment)
Tier 2	Preferred brand-name drugs	$20 - $40 (moderate copayment)
Tier 3	Non-preferred brand-name drugs	$40 - $100+ (higher copayment or coinsurance)
Tier 4	Specialty drugs	25% - 33% coinsurance or higher

Additional Cost Considerations

- **Deductible:** You may have to pay a deductible with some Part D plans before the plan will start paying for your medicines. Plan deductibles for Part D drugs go up to $545 in 2024, but many plans have lower deductibles, and some don't have any at all for lower-tier drugs.
- **Coverage Gap (Donut Hole):** A beneficiary joins the coverage gap (also called the donut hole) when their total drug costs, which are paid for by both them and their plan, hit a certain amount ($5,030 in 2024). During this time, people who get drugs pay 25% of the cost of both brand-name and generic drugs. In the past few years, the funding gap has slowly closed, but recipients may still have to pay more out of pocket at this point.
- **Catastrophic Coverage:** The user enters the catastrophic coverage phase when their out-of-pocket drug costs hit a certain amount ($8,000 in 2024). For the rest of the year, they only pay a small coinsurance or copayment. At this point, Medicare pays for most of the drugs.

Formulary Management and Changes

It is important to know that Medicare Part D plans can change their formulary at any time during the year. However, plans must let beneficiaries know about any changes that might affect the drugs they are taking. Drugs can be changed from one tier to another, taken off the formulary, or given new restrictions about how they can be used.

Utilization Management Tools

To keep costs down and make sure that medicines are used correctly, many plans use utilization management tools like
- **Prior Authorization:** The plan requires approval before covering certain drugs.
- **Quantity Limits:** These are limits on how much of a drug will be paid for in a certain amount of time.
- **Step Therapy:** Before covering a more expensive drug, the plan may require beneficiaries to try drugs that cost less.

The Medicare Annual Enrollment Period (AEP) is when people can ask for an exception or switch to a different plan if their drug isn't covered or is limited in one of these ways.

Choosing a Part D Plan Based on Formulary Tiers

It's important to review the formulary and know where your medicines fit in the tier system before choosing a Medicare Part D plan. Take a look at this:

- **Check Coverage:** Make sure that your plan's formulary covers the medicines you take. You might have to pay full price for your medications if they are not.
- **Compare Costs:** Look at how much each tier of medicine costs. It's important to look at the total cost of coverage because a plan with a smaller payment might have higher out-of-pocket costs for medicines.
- **Look at the Deductible:** The deductible may only apply to more expensive drugs in some plans, but it may apply to all drugs in others. Think about how this will change your costs.
- **Utilization Management:** Check to see if any of your medicines need to be approved first, go through step treatment, or have time or amount limits. These rules may make it harder for you to get to your medicines.

Coverage Gap (Donut Hole) and How It Works

People who talk about Medicare use the phrase donut hole to describe a funding gap in the Part D prescription drug benefit. People who signed up for Part D used to pay their premium plus out-of-pocket copayments up to a certain point. In the next phase, called the donut hole, they had to pay full price for drugs that were reimbursed until their out-of-pocket costs hit a certain amount. After that, people who had signed up for coverage moved into the catastrophic phase, where they had low copayments that lowered the cost of their drugs. For new enrollees, the cost-sharing in the donut hole is now similar to what they pay during the initial coverage phase. In both stages, individuals are responsible for 25% of the cost for both brand-name and generic medications. Additionally, they must cover a 25% dispensing fee, which typically adds $1 to $3 for each prescription refill.

Medicare Part D phases

The following are the Medicare Part D phases and cost-sharing:
- **Deductible or initial phase:** For the first few months, after January 1, you pay the full price for your medicines until your deductible is met, if you have one. In 2024, the standard Part D deductible can't be more than $545. At this point, your plan doesn't pay anything.
- **Initial coverage (post-deductible) phase:** Once you've paid your deductible, your plan will start to share the costs with you. You pay 25% (or up to $1,257.50 if your plan doesn't have a deductible), and your plan pays 75%. At this time, your plan pays up to $3,772.50. In 2024, the first amount of coverage for plans with a fee will be $5,030. This amount includes the amounts that you and your plan pay.
- **Donut hole (coverage gap) phase:** The donut hole (coverage gap) phase means that you still have to pay 25% of the cost of your drugs and 25% of the pharmacy's handling fee. This means that you have to pay an extra $1 to $3 for each prescription fill. Generic drugs will cost you 75% less than brand-name drugs because of your health plan. Your insurance will pay 5% of the cost of brand-name drugs, and a maker discount will cover the other 70%. Before you can get out of the donut hole, you'll need to be charged with paying $8,000 in 2024. This includes the amounts you and other groups, like Extra Help, have paid on your behalf, as well as the value of maker discounts.
- **Catastrophic (post-donut hole) phase:** When you hit the catastrophic phase (after the donut hole), you won't have to pay for your medicines out of pocket after 2024.

When do you enter the Medicare Part D coverage gap?

When you've used up all of your starting coverage, you hit the donut hole. In 2024, you stay there until your out-of-pocket prices and third-party spending hit $8,000.

Costs in the coverage gap

It's still up to you to pay up to 25% of the price of most prescription drugs during the coverage gap. However, your health plan's payment for brand-name drugs changes from the beginning of coverage. You won't have to pay more than 25% of the cost of your prescriptions out of pocket after 2024; this could cost a lot, depending on the medicines you take. As was already said, you won't be able to get out of the donut hole until your out-of-pocket spending for the year reaches $8,000. This includes any savings you get on brand-name medicines and the amount paid for you by outside groups, like Extra Help. When you're in the donut hole, your health plan's payments for your drugs don't count toward your $8,000 limit like they did when you first started coverage.

Brand-name drugs

When purchasing medications at a pharmacy or through a mail-order service, you are responsible for a 25% cost-sharing fee. Some plans may offer even lower prices if the pharmacy agrees to reduce the set price for specific medications. **Here's how nearly the full cost of the drug is applied to your out-of-pocket expenses:**

- The drug manufacturer covers 70% of the cost as a discount.
- Your plan contributes 5% of the cost.
- You pay 25% of the drug's cost.
- Additionally, there is a dispensing fee, with your plan covering 75% of it and you paying 25%, which usually amounts to $1 to $3 per prescription.

However, the portion your drug plan covers is not counted toward your out-of-pocket expenses.

Generic drugs

The price for brand-name drugs works in a different way than the policy for generic drugs. General drugs will cost you 25% more than your Part D plan, which will cover 75% of the cost. You will only get out of the coverage gap if you pay enough for generic drugs.

How do you get out of the Medicare Part D donut hole?

When your credited out-of-pocket bills hit $8,000 in 2024, you'll be out of the donut hole. This amount includes the value of producer savings as well as the money you and other groups, like Extra Help, have paid for things.

Expenses that count toward the coverage gap

These expenses count toward the coverage gap:

- Your yearly deductible, coinsurance, and copayments
- The discount you get on brand-name drugs in the coverage gap
- The amount you pay in the coverage gap

Expenses that don't count toward the coverage gap

These expenses do not count toward the coverage gap:

- Your drug plan premium
- Pharmacy dispensing fee
- The amount you pay for drugs that aren't covered

Is there any insurance that can cover you while you're in the donut hole?

Not at all. In the donut hole, no insurance can help you pay for things. It is important to know that some Medigap or Medicare supplement plans only cover Parts A and B of Medicare when it comes to premiums, coinsurance, and copayments.

What you can do

Medicare's Part D Low-Income Subsidy, also known as Extra Help, helps people who are having trouble paying their Part D fees, deductibles, or copayments by giving them money. The donut hole doesn't affect people who get Extra Help. In 2023, you may be able to get Extra Help if you make up to $21,870 a year ($29,580 for a married couple) and have up to $16,600 in assets ($33,240 for a married couple). You can fill out a form on the Social Security website to find out if you are eligible. (There were no numbers for 2024 available at the time this article was written, but they should be added later.) You can sign up for Part D no matter when your initial or special registration time ends if you get Extra Help. There are no late enrollment fees. Extra Help helps pay your Part D monthly fees, yearly deductibles, and copayments for your medicines. To get Extra Help, you can either go online or call the Social Security Administration at 1-800-772-1213. As was already said, you can sign up for Extra Help and look for other ways to save money. If you use savings, like the ones GoodRx gives you, the prices may go down to less than your Medicare Part D drug fee. Also, some drug companies have programs that let people who can't afford their medicines get them for little or no cost. It's possible to move to a different prescription drug plan when it's time for Medicare open enrollment. Take some time to look at different plans, and pick the one whose menu has lower copayments for the medicines you need. Also, look at the pharmacies that your plan recommends; usually, these pharmacies have arranged lower drug prices.

The bottom line

The amount you spend on prescription medications each year plays a significant role in determining your overall Medicare Part D costs. Medicare Part D operates in stages, starting with the deductible phase, followed by the initial coverage phase, and then moving into what is commonly known as the "donut hole" or coverage gap. In 2024, you will enter the coverage gap once the combined spending between you and your Medicare Part D plan reaches $5,030 on prescription drugs. At this point, the way costs are shared between you and your plan changes. While in the donut hole, you are responsible for paying no more than 25% of the cost of your medications, in addition to 25% of the pharmacy's dispensing fee, which typically ranges from $1 to $3. For generic medications, your health plan covers 75% of the cost. For brand-name drugs, your Part D plan pays 5% of the cost, while the manufacturer covers 70% of the expense, leaving you with 25% of the remaining cost. You exit the coverage gap once your total out-of-pocket spending, including what you've paid for medications and certain other costs, reaches $8,000 in 2024. It's important to note that the payments made by your Part D plan while you're in the donut hole do not count toward your out-of-pocket limit. After you've reached the out-of-pocket threshold, you enter the "catastrophic coverage" phase. During this phase, your Medicare Part D plan will cover most of the remaining prescription costs for the rest of the year, significantly reducing your financial burden. For individuals receiving **Extra Help** (a program that assists low-income beneficiaries with prescription costs), the donut hole will not apply after 2024. Extra Help recipients will receive financial assistance to cover their medications, ensuring continuous affordability throughout the year.

CHAPTER 3
MEDICARE ENROLLMENT PROCESS

Initial Enrollment Period (IEP)

This is a seven-month window during which individuals can enroll in Medicare Part A (hospital insurance) and Part B (medical insurance) under Original Medicare. This enrollment period is unique to each person, based on their 65th birthday, and is independent of other Medicare enrollment periods. Your IEP begins three months before your 65th birthday, includes your birthday month, and extends for three months afterward. For example, if you were born on September 16, your IEP would run from June 1 to December 31. It's a critical time to ensure you enroll in Medicare to avoid any late enrollment penalties. In special cases, such as those with qualifying disabilities or certain health conditions, you may be eligible to enroll in Medicare before reaching age 65. Although Medicare is managed by the Centers for Medicare & Medicaid Services (CMS), the Social Security Administration (SSA) handles the enrollment process. For more information or to begin the enrollment process, visit SSA.gov.

How to Prepare for the Medicare IEP

The first step in preparing for your Medicare IEP is marking your calendar with the specific dates of your enrollment window. However, this is just the beginning of understanding your Medicare choices and making the most of your benefits. Next, familiarize yourself with the different parts of Medicare (A, B, C, and D) and how they function together. Starting your research early will ensure that you're confident in your choices when your IEP begins, avoiding any penalties or gaps in coverage. A helpful resource to get started is the "Checklist for Online Medicare Applications" available on the Social Security Administration's website. This checklist will guide you in gathering the necessary information and documents needed for a smooth application process.

Automatic Enrollment

If you are already receiving Social Security or Railroad Retirement Board benefits before you turn 65, you will be automatically enrolled in Medicare Parts A and B. Your coverage will start on the first day of the month you turn 65, and you should receive your Medicare card by mail up to three months before your coverage begins. If you're not receiving Social Security or Railroad Retirement Board benefits, you will need to manually sign up during your IEP. To ensure coverage starts promptly on the first of your birthday month, it's recommended to sign up during the first three months of your IEP.

Working Past Age 65

If you or your spouse plans to continue working after age 65 and have health insurance through an employer, you may need to consider how Medicare works alongside your group health plan. Depending on your existing coverage, you may choose to delay enrolling in Medicare Part B. In some cases, your employer-sponsored group health plan will remain your primary insurance, with Medicare acting as secondary coverage. Before making any decisions, consult with your employer's benefits administrator to understand how Medicare integrates with your current health coverage and what options are available.

Understanding Coverage Options

While Original Medicare provides a robust foundation for healthcare coverage, it may not cover all the services you or your spouse might need. Medicare Part A covers hospital stays, nursing facility care, hospice care, and some home health services. Part B covers preventive care, doctor visits, and outpatient treatments. After enrolling in Original Medicare, you can choose to enhance your coverage by adding private insurance options. Medicare Part C (Medicare Advantage) combines the benefits of Parts A and B, and often includes additional services such as dental, hearing, and vision care. Some Medicare Advantage plans, known as MAPDs, also include prescription drug coverage (Part D).

What Happens if I Miss My Initial Enrollment Period?

If you miss your Initial Enrollment Period, there are other opportunities to enroll in Medicare throughout the year. The three main enrollment periods are:
- **Initial Enrollment Period (IEP)**: The first window tied to your 65th birthday.
- **Special Enrollment Period (SEP)**: This is available under specific circumstances, such as losing Medicaid coverage, moving, or experiencing a major disaster. The start and end dates of an SEP vary based on the individual's situation, and enrollment during this period typically avoids late penalties.
- **Annual Enrollment Period (AEP)**: If you miss both the IEP and SEP, you can enroll in Medicare during the AEP, which occurs each year from October 15 to December 7. Keep in mind that enrolling during this period may result in late enrollment penalties.

Understanding the various enrollment periods can help ensure you avoid unnecessary costs and maintain continuous health coverage.

General Enrollment Period (GEP)

People can sign up for Medicare during the General Enrollment Period (GEP), which runs from January 1 to March 31 every year. This is the only time that people who are qualified for Medicare Parts A and/or B but did not sign up when they were first eligible can do so. People who skipped any Special Enrollment Periods (SEPs) can also sign up for Parts A and/or B, which is also known as basic Medicare.

When is the first opportunity to join Medicare Parts A and/or B?

People can usually sign up for Medicare for the first time during their Initial Enrollment Period (IEP). This period begins three months before a person turns 65, or after two years if they've been getting Social Security Disability Insurance (SSDI) for 24 months before turning 65. In months 21 or 22, they should get their Welcome to Medicare kit. Most people who are still working after age 65 and get their health insurance through their workplace (or a spouse who is still working) can safely wait to sign up for Medicare Part B during the Initial Enrollment Period until the worker quits. However, there may be a late registration charge for people who don't sign up for Medicare Parts A and B on time and don't have other insurance through work. Most of the time, people who are eligible for Medicare Part A take it when they first become qualified. Most people don't have to pay a monthly premium for Part A because they pay for it through payroll taxes while they're working. However, some people are eligible for Medicare Part A but did not work long enough under our Social Security system to be eligible for premium-free Part A. These people can still join Medicare, but they have to pay a voluntary Part A monthly premium. During the Initial Enrollment Period (IEP), the only individuals who can safely delay enrolling in Medicare Part B without facing a late enrollment penalty are those still employed after turning 65. They must also receive health insurance through their job, which covers them, their Medicare-eligible spouse, and any adult disabled children who live with them and rely on them for support. These individuals can wait to sign up for Part B until the employed person retires.

Why would someone delay Part B enrollment?

- It would be smart to wait until the worker retires since the employer's health insurance generally pays first and then Medicare. Also, it doesn't leave much room for Medicare Part B payment most of the time.
- If your clients have Medicare Part B, the first six months are the best time to buy a Medicare supplement (Medigap) policy because it's the cheapest and there is no medical screening or pre-existing condition limits.

For most people who continue working past 65 and have employer-provided health insurance, it's common to wait to enroll in Part B until they are nearing retirement. This is known as a Special Enrollment Period. For most individuals, it's highly recommended to sign up for Medicare Parts A and B as soon as they're eligible to avoid missing important deadlines. However, sometimes people don't enroll during this initial period, and they may need another opportunity to join. The General Enrollment Period (GEP) provides an alternative for individuals who missed their Initial Enrollment Period (IEP).

How the General Enrollment Period Works

The General Enrollment Period runs from January 1 to March 31 each year. During this window, anyone who is eligible for Medicare but has not yet enrolled can do so. The coverage, however, will only start the month following their enrollment, regardless of which parts of Medicare they choose to sign up for during the GEP. One important consideration for those who delayed signing up for Medicare Part B is the potential late enrollment penalty. If someone waits more than a year after becoming eligible for Part B, they may face a penalty added to their monthly premiums. This penalty is calculated at 10% of the standard Part B premium for every full year they delayed enrollment. **This additional cost continues as long as they have Medicare Part B, unless they fall into specific categories such as:**

- Qualifying for a Medicare Savings Program (MSP) that covers Part B premiums, or
- Becoming eligible for Medicare due to a disability, receiving a penalty, but later turning 65. In this case, the penalty may be waived.

Similarly, individuals who are eligible for premium-based Medicare Part A but delay enrolling could also face a late penalty. For Part A, the penalty amounts to an extra 10% of the premium, but it only applies for a period equal to double the number of years they delayed signing up. Additionally, certain groups, such as those who qualify for the Qualified Medicare Beneficiary (QMB) Program, might have this penalty removed once they turn 65.

Why the General Enrollment Period is Crucial for Low-Income Individuals

Low-income individuals often forgo enrolling in Medicare Part B during their IEP due to the high costs involved, or they may choose not to enroll in premium-based Part A. Fortunately, there are programs, such as Medicare Savings Programs, that can help cover Part B costs, potentially saving clients from having to worry about late penalties. For example, three primary Medicare

Savings Programs assist in covering Part B premiums. Some states will even enroll eligible individuals in Medicare Part B at any time throughout the year under the Medicare Savings Program umbrella.

Using the QMB Program to Enroll in Part A

To receive help through Medicare Savings Programs, individuals must first enroll in Medicare Part A. If they don't automatically qualify for premium-free Part A, they can take advantage of the QMB program, which covers the cost of the Part A premium. The enrollment process starts by visiting a local Social Security Administration office to sign up for Medicare Part A. For those interested in enrolling in Part A but only if QMB will cover the premium, they can request a "conditional enrollment." In this scenario, their Part A enrollment will only be processed if they qualify for QMB. After receiving the necessary documents from Social Security, clients must take this paperwork to their local Medicaid office, along with an application for the Medicare Savings Program. Since this process can be complicated, having a benefits counselor assist clients can help ensure the process goes smoothly.

Conditional Enrollment Timing and the GEP

In most states, conditional enrollment for Part A can occur any time throughout the year. However, in 14 states, including Alabama, Arizona, and Colorado, and Illinois, conditional enrollment is limited to the GEP window. For those in these states, the GEP represents a critical time to assist individuals who are eligible for Medicare but has not yet enrolled—particularly those who qualify for programs like QMB.

Special Enrollment Period for Medicare Part D

Enrolling in Medicare during the General Enrollment Period also opens up a Special Enrollment Period (SEP) for Medicare Part D, which covers prescription drugs. Once a person signs up for Medicare Parts A or B during the GEP, they can use this SEP to enroll in a Part D plan. The SEP lasts for two months, starting the month after enrolling in Part A or B. Coverage under Part D begins the month following the Part D enrollment, ensuring timely access to prescription medication.

Special Enrollment Period (SEP)

A Special Enrollment Period (SEP) allows individuals to enroll in or modify their qualified health plans (QHPs) outside of the standard Open Enrollment Period (OEP). SEPs are typically triggered by specific life events, such as changes in family status, employment, or other significant circumstances. These life events may include getting married, losing health coverage, or moving to a new area with different health plan options. In some cases, even during the annual OEP, certain individuals may qualify for a SEP—such as when they have a child or experience other major life changes. This can be especially beneficial; as it enables coverage to start sooner than if they had waited for the regular enrollment process without the SEP. For those who meet the criteria, the SEP offers an important opportunity to adjust or obtain coverage without having to wait for the next OEP, ensuring they can maintain continuous health coverage.

Events that permit a Special Enrollment Period include:
- Loss of qualifying health coverage (Note: This SEP does not include loss of coverage due to nonpayment of premiums)
- Change in household size
- Change in the primary place of living that results in access to new QHPs
- Change in eligibility for Marketplace coverage or help to pay for coverage
- Enrollment or plan error
- Estimated annual household income below 150% of the federal poverty level (FPL)
- Loss of Medicaid or Children's Health Insurance Program (CHIP) coverage between March 31, 2023, and November 30, 2024
- Other situations and exceptional circumstances

Most of the time, people have 60 days from the date of the qualified event to sign up for coverage. People who are part of a nationally recognized Indian group or an Alaska Native Claims Settlement Act (ANCSA) Corporation can change or sign up for a plan once a month, 365 days a year, without having to go through another qualified life event.

Late Enrollment Penalties and How to Avoid Them

Medicare isn't always easy to understand. Because of this, a lot of people don't know how or when to sign up. You could be fined for life if you don't sign up for Medicare on time, so it's important to know your Initial Enrollment Period and work with a registered Medicare expert to make sure you get the right coverage at the right time. The good news is that fees for leaving Medicare late are easy to avoid if you know how they work. Find out about the punishments for each Part by reading on. Please do not be afraid to call us whenever you have a question. Our help is always free.

Medicare Part A Late Enrollment Penalty

Most Americans receive Medicare Part A without paying premiums, and there is no penalty for signing up late, regardless of when you choose to enroll. However, if neither you nor your spouse worked and paid taxes for at least 10 years, missing your Initial Enrollment Period (IEP) may result in a penalty. If this happens, you'll need to wait until the General Enrollment Period (January 1–March 31 each year) to sign up, and you'll face a penalty on top of your premium. The penalty is 10% of the monthly premium, and you'll have to pay it for twice the number of years you delayed enrolling. For example, if you missed your IEP but sign up during the next General Enrollment Period, you'll need to pay the penalty for two years.

How to Avoid the Medicare Part A Late Enrollment Penalty

If you're approaching age 65, you have a seven-month period to enroll in Medicare. This window starts three months before your 65th birthday, includes the month of your birthday, and extends for three months afterward. It's crucial to make sure you're enrolled in Medicare Part A during this period. You can confirm your enrollment by receiving your red, white, and blue Medicare card, checking your Medicare or Social Security account online, or contacting the Social Security Administration directly. If you haven't been automatically enrolled, it's essential to call Social Security to get signed up and avoid any penalties for late enrollment.

Medicare Part B Late Enrollment Penalty

Failing to sign up for Medicare Part B during your Initial Enrollment Period (IEP) and not qualifying for a Special Enrollment Period (SEP) can result in a permanent penalty. This penalty adds an extra 10% to your monthly Part B premium for every full year that you delayed enrollment. For instance, if you sign up two years late without qualifying for an SEP, you'll pay an additional 20% on top of your standard Part B premium for as long as you have Medicare.

How to Avoid the Part B Late Enrollment Penalty

The Part B penalty can become a significant financial burden, particularly for those living on fixed incomes. To prevent this, it's important to know your IEP and whether you qualify for a SEP. If you're unsure about qualifying for a SEP, it's better to sign up during your IEP to avoid any penalties. However, if you believe you're eligible for a SEP, you may choose to wait, but it's worth comparing your current healthcare coverage with what Medicare Part B offers to ensure you're making the most cost-effective decision.

Medicare Part D Late Enrollment Penalty

While Medicare Part D, which covers prescription drugs, is optional, not enrolling when you first qualify can lead to a late enrollment penalty if you decide to join later. The Part D penalty is based on the number of months you went without credible prescription drug coverage and is calculated using the national base beneficiary premium. This amount changes annually, and in 2024, it is $34.70. For example, if you went 14 months without coverage, the penalty would be approximately $4.90 per month, which is added to your Part D premium. This penalty remains as long as you have a Part D plan. If you're receiving Extra Help, a program designed to assist low-income individuals with prescription drug costs, you won't have to pay this penalty.

How to Avoid the Part D Late Enrollment Penalty

To avoid the Part D late enrollment penalty, it's best to enroll when you first sign up for Medicare, even if you're not currently taking prescription medications. Opting for a low-cost plan can help ensure you're covered if your medication needs change. **Additionally, you can avoid the penalty if:**
- You don't go without creditable prescription drug coverage for more than 63 days.
- You choose not to enroll in a Part D or Medicare Advantage plan at all.

Does Medicare Advantage (Part C) Have a Late Enrollment Penalty?

Medicare Advantage plans, which are alternatives to Original Medicare (Parts A and B), do not have late enrollment penalties. This is because you must already be enrolled in Original Medicare to qualify for Medicare Advantage. You can enroll in a Medicare Advantage plan during your Initial Enrollment Period or wait for the Annual Enrollment Period, which runs from October 15 to December 7 each year.

Does Medigap (Medicare Supplement) Have a Late Enrollment Penalty?

Medigap, or Medicare Supplement Insurance, helps cover costs that Original Medicare doesn't pay, such as coinsurance and deductibles. While there's no late enrollment penalty for Medigap, there are potential drawbacks to enrolling after your Initial Enrollment Period. The Medigap Open Enrollment Period lasts for six months after you first sign up for Medicare Part B. During this time, insurance companies must offer you coverage regardless of your health status. If you try to enroll after this period, you may face medical underwriting, and insurers could deny coverage based on pre-existing conditions. Therefore, enrolling in a Medigap plan during the Open Enrollment Period offers the most protection and flexibility.

Other Special Enrollment Periods: Medicare Late Enrollment Penalty Exceptions

Individuals who are still covered by their employer's health insurance or prefer their group health plan can delay enrolling in Medicare without incurring penalties. They can take advantage of a Special Enrollment Period (SEP) once they stop working or their group coverage ends. Enrolling during this SEP allows them to bypass the late enrollment fees that normally apply when someone signs up for Medicare after the Initial Enrollment Period (IEP) has passed. There are additional situations where you may qualify for a SEP and avoid the late enrollment penalty. **These include specific life events such as:**

- Losing eligibility for Medicaid.
- Receiving incorrect or misleading information from your health plan or employer that caused you to miss your Medicare enrollment window.
- Being affected by a natural disaster, which disrupted your ability to sign up.
- Being recently released from incarceration.
- Moving to a new location outside of the coverage area for your Medicare drug plan or Medicare Advantage plan.

If none of these situations apply, but you believe you should qualify for a Special Enrollment Period, it's possible to contact Social Security and explain your circumstances. In many cases, they may grant an exception to avoid late penalties. We can also assist you in determining whether you qualify for a SEP and guide you through the enrollment process.

Why Does Medicare Have Enrollment Penalties?

Medicare isn't the simplest program to understand, and penalties for not enrolling can make older Americans scared since they are already worried about retirement money. You may be asking why there are fines for not enrolling in the first place. Medicare late enrollment fines are in place to make sure that a lot of people pay their bills. For insurance companies to be able to meet the wants of everyone, they need a lot of members, especially healthy people. This means that if everyone only signed up for insurance when they needed it, they wouldn't have enough money to pay for everyone who needed care.

How to Sign Up for Medicare (Online, Phone, and In-Person)

You can apply for Medicare online if you:

- Are within the 7-month initial enrollment window
- Live in the U.S. or one of its territories

Remember that you can apply for Medicare online too, even if you don't want to start getting regular Social Security benefits just yet. SSA.gov, which is the official SSA website, is the only place online where you can sign up for real Medicare. You can start a new application for Medicare at www.ssa.gov if you are ready to sign up and are qualified. Even though the SSA decides who is eligible for Medicare, you don't have to be getting Social Security to get

Medicare. A quick and easy way to sign up for Medicare is online registration. The application shouldn't take more than 30 minutes to finish, and you don't have to do it all at once. As long as you don't lose your work, you can start and stop your application. Click **Submit Now** when you're done with the application to send it to the SSA. After that, you'll be given an application number that will let you know how your registration is going. If you want to sign up for original Medicare, make sure you do it through SSA.gov. Other websites may say they can help you sign up for Medicare, but what they do is take your information to use for marketing. You won't be signed up.

Steps to Sign Up Online

1. Create an Account and Register

To sign up for Medicare, you'll need to visit the **Social Security Administration's website**. Although it may seem unrelated, the Social Security site is where you complete your Medicare enrollment. Once there, choose the option to apply online for Medicare from the available registration methods. After that, review and agree to the terms of service, then click **Next** to continue the process.

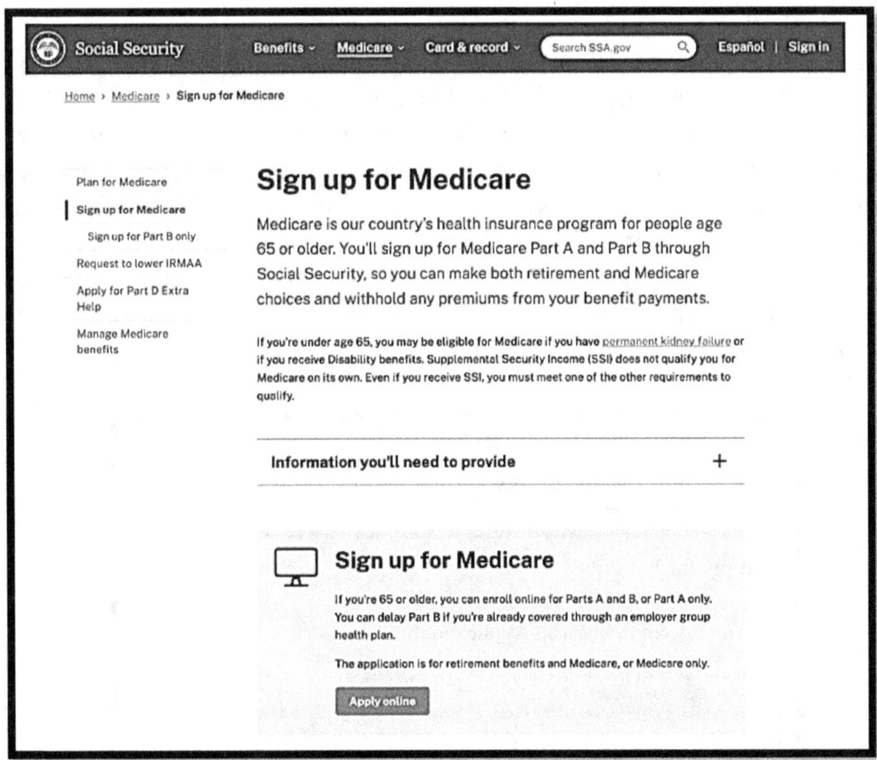

2. Apply for benefits.

On this screen, under **Apply & Complete**, click the **Start a New Application** button.

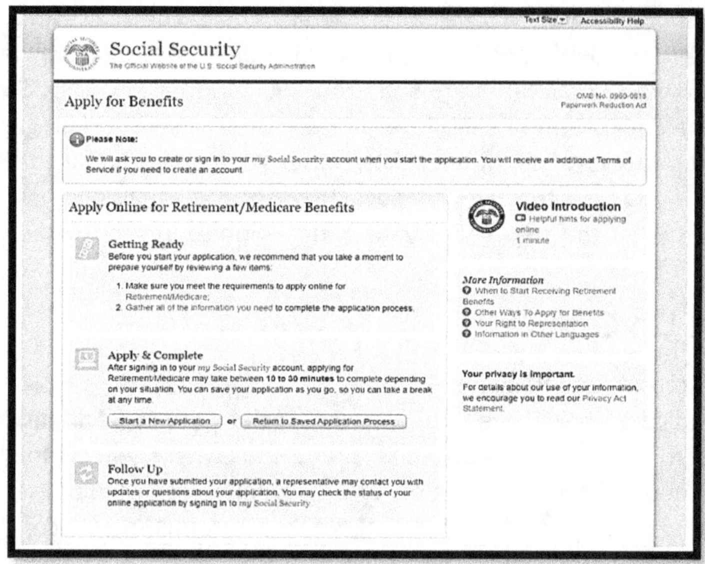

Social Security
The Official Website of the U.S. Social Security Administration

Apply for Benefits

OMB No. 0960-0618
Paperwork Reduction Act

Please Note:
We will ask you to create or sign in to your *my* Social Security account when you start the application. You will receive an additional Terms of Service if you need to create an account

Apply Online for Retirement/Medicare Benefits

Getting Ready
Before you start your application, we recommend that you take a moment to prepare yourself by reviewing a few items:

1. Make sure you meet the requirements to apply online for Retirement/Medicare;
2. Gather all of the information you need to complete the application process.

Apply & Complete
After signing in to your *my* Social Security account, applying for Retirement/Medicare may take between **10 to 30 minutes** to complete depending on your situation. You can save your application as you go, so you can take a break at any time.

[Start a New Application] or [Return to Saved Application Process]

Follow Up
Once you have submitted your application, a representative may contact you with updates or questions about your application. You may check the status of your online application by signing in to *my* Social Security

Video Introduction
Helpful hints for applying online
1 minute

More Information
When to Start Receiving Retirement Benefits
Other Ways To Apply for Benefits
Your Right to Representation
Information in Other Languages

Your privacy is important.
For details about our use of your information, we encourage you to read our Privacy Act Statement.

Text Size ▾   Accessibility Help

3. Indicate whether or not you already have a Social Security account.

You'll have to sign in if you do. If not, you'll have to create one. You should also have your driver's license and social security number on hand. One of two ways will be asked of you to prove who you are: live-chat with a video agent or hit a button that sends a link to your phone. You can use that link to send pictures of the front and back of your driver's license and a digital selfie to prove who you are. For the second one, you'll need to take your glasses off and hold your phone up to your face. If any of this seems too hard or you don't have the right tools, you can always call Social Security at 1-800-772-1213 (TTY users should call 1-800-325-0778) to make an appointment to apply in person. You can also call the Social Security office in your area here. There may be long wait times, both on the phone and in person.

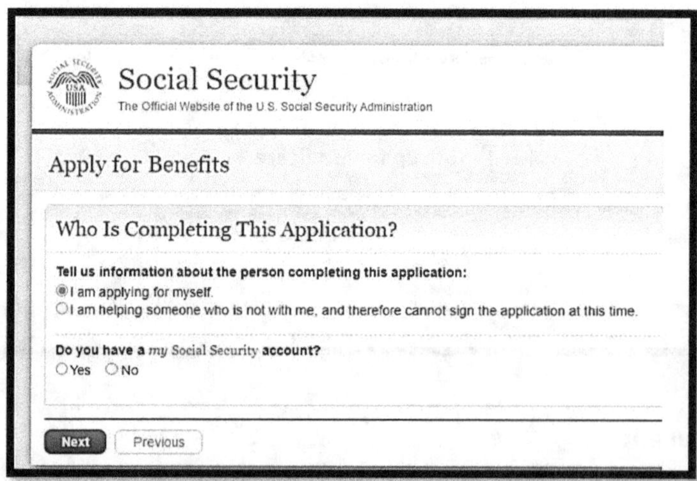

Social Security
The Official Website of the U.S. Social Security Administration

Apply for Benefits

Who Is Completing This Application?

Tell us information about the person completing this application:
◉ I am applying for myself.
○ I am helping someone who is not with me, and therefore cannot sign the application at this time.

Do you have a *my* Social Security **account?**
○ Yes   ○ No

[Next]   [Previous]

4. **Log in** to your **Social Security account**.

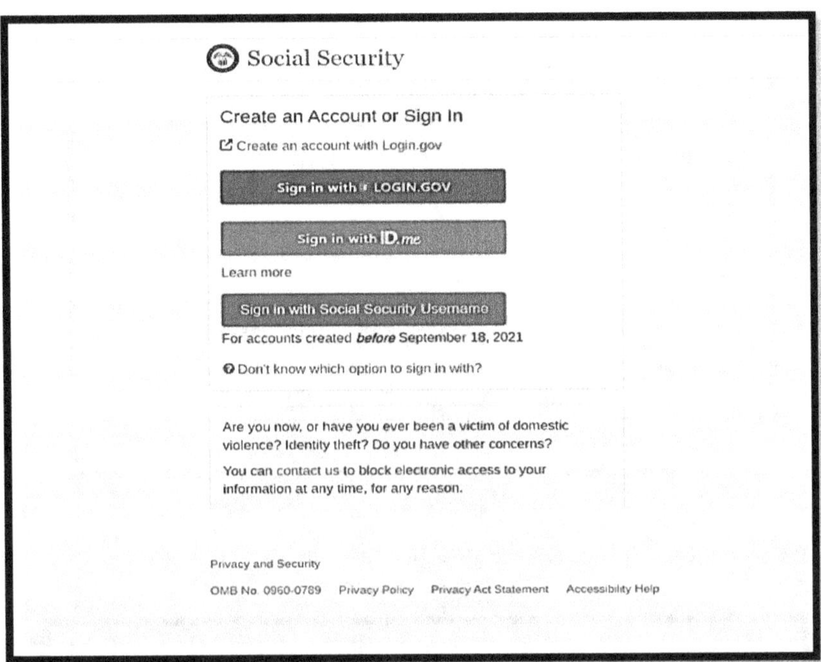

5. Give some personal details, like your name, social security number, date of birth, danger, and so on.

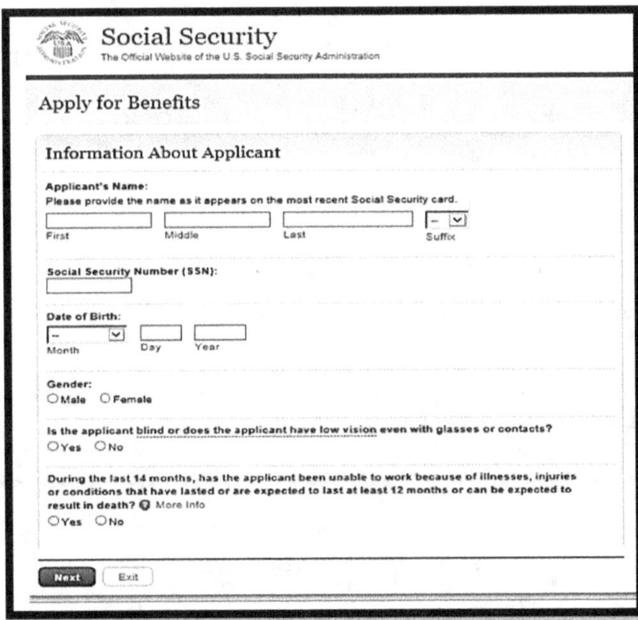

6. Answer the question on the next screen.

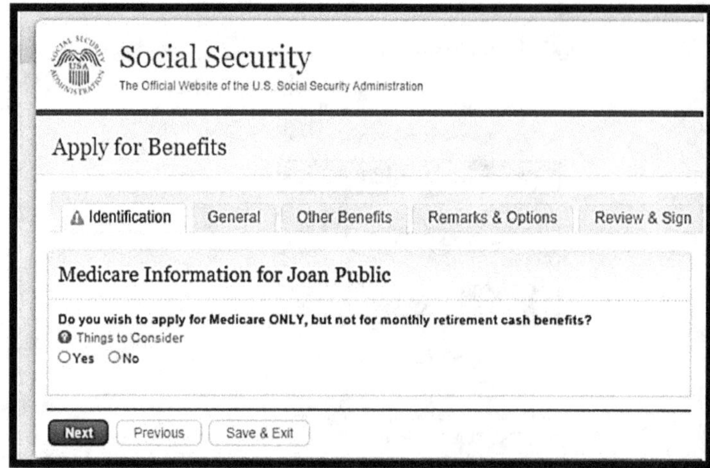

7. You can choose to join Medicare Part B if you want to.

8. Give details about your other insurance, if you have any.

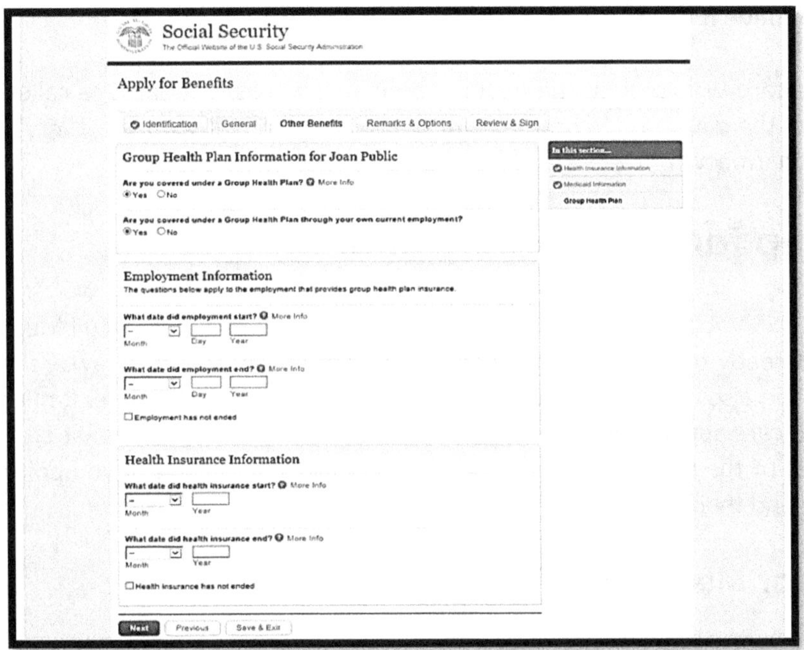

9. When you're ready, sign the application and submit it.

NOTE: After you click **Submit Now**, you won't be able to change anything in your application.

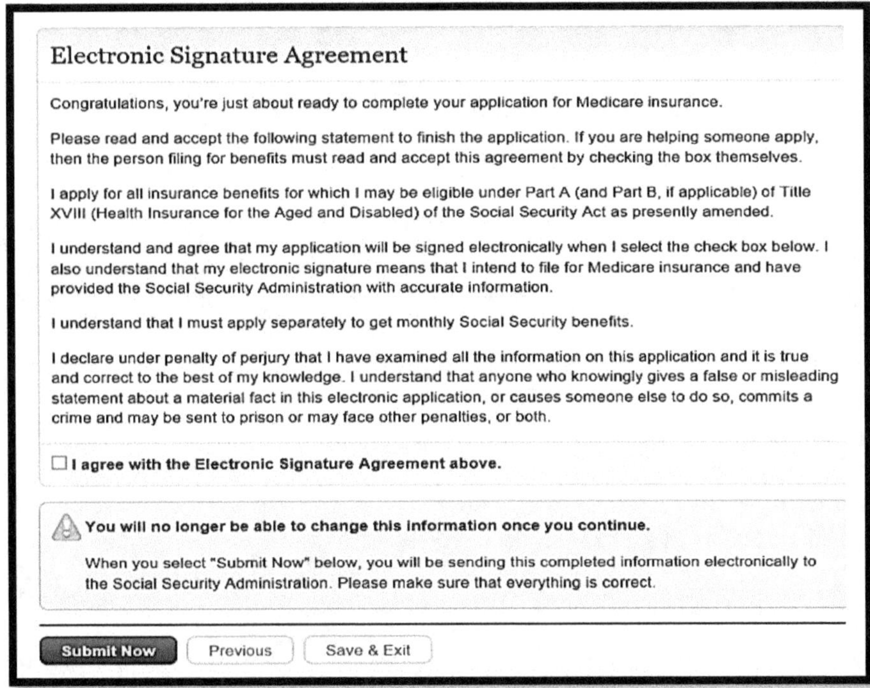

Good job! You made it through!

Your Medicare card will come in the mail in about two weeks in a package called **Welcome to Medicare**. As of the date printed on the front of the card, bring it with you every time you go to the doctor or pharmacy.

Signing up for Medicare by phone

You can call the SSA at 1-800-772-1213 (TTY 1-800-325-0778) to apply for full Medicare over the phone, but get ready to wait. It's possible that you won't get help right away if someone else calls first. You can also make plans for a phone interview on your own time. It might take longer to process Medicare applications that are sent over the phone than those that are sent online or in person. Most of the time, you have to wait for forms to be mailed to you before you can fill them out and send them back.

Applying for Medicare in person

To sign up for Medicare in person, you can visit the SSA office in your area. In case you need to send in your application quickly because you will be 65 soon, this is a good choice.

CHAPTER 4
COSTS ASSOCIATED WITH MEDICARE

Medicare pays for everything, from yearly checkups to visits to the emergency room. That doesn't mean the care is free, though; you will have to pay some of the bills whether you are 65 or older or younger and have an eligible condition. Knowing how much the care you need will cost you out of pocket can help you make sure you can pay for it.

How much does Medicare typically cost?

Medicare costs change based on the type of plan you choose and the amount of care you get through it. Every year, the federal government changes the fees, deductibles, and payments for Medicare.

How much Medicare costs will go up in 2024

This 2024, Medicare costs will change a little. Take a look at some of the changes below.

Medicare Cost	2023 Cost	2024 Cost
Part A Premium	$0 for most, others pay $278 or $506/month (based on tax quarters)	$0 for most, others pay $278 or $505/month (based on tax quarters)
Part A Hospital Deductible	$1,600 per benefit period	$1,632 per benefit period
Part B Premium	$164.90/month for most, up to $560.50 for higher incomes	$174.70/month for most, up to $594 for higher incomes
Part B Deductible	$226 per year	$240 per year
Part D Coverage Gap Begins	$4,660 spent	$5,030 spent
Part D Catastrophic Coverage Begins	$7,400 spent	$8,000 spent

How much does the average Medicare beneficiary spend out of pocket?

A 2016 study by the Kaiser Family Foundation (KFF) revealed that individuals with Original Medicare typically spent over $5,000 annually, which breaks down to more than $400 per month. Similarly, a 2019 spending survey from AARP found that the average person with standard Medicare incurred $6,663 per year on insurance and healthcare expenses. However, your actual costs can vary based on your specific healthcare needs and circumstances. One key difference to keep in mind is that Original Medicare does not have a cap on out-of-pocket spending unless you have additional coverage like a Medigap plan. In contrast, Medicare Advantage (MA) plans offer the benefit of out-of-pocket spending limits, providing more **financial protection for those who enroll. In 2024, the maximum out-of-pocket limits for MA plans are:**

- $8,850 for in-network services
- $13,300 for combined in-network and out-of-network services

For assistance with choosing coverage, the State Health Insurance Assistance Program (SHIP) offers free, unbiased counseling to help you understand your Medicare options.

How much are Medicare premiums?

When you're enrolled in Medicare, the amount you pay each month for coverage is referred to as a **premium**. These premiums, specifically for Medicare Parts A and B, are determined by the federal government and are updated every year. Medicare Advantage (also known as Part C) and Part D (prescription drug coverage) premiums, on the other hand, are offered by private insurance companies, so they can vary from plan to plan and year to year.

Medicare Part A (Hospital Insurance)

For most people, **Part A** comes at no additional monthly cost. This is typically the case if you or your spouse have worked and paid Medicare taxes for at least 10 years. However, if you haven't accumulated enough work credits, you might need to pay a monthly premium, which in 2024 is either **$278** or **$505**, depending on your contribution history.

Medicare Part B (Medical Insurance)

For **Part B**, most beneficiaries will pay a monthly premium of **$174.70** in 2024. However, if your income exceeds certain thresholds, you might be required to pay a higher premium—up to **$594** per month.

Medicare Part C (Medicare Advantage)

Medicare Advantage (Part C) plans offer an alternative to Original Medicare, bundling both Parts A and B and often including additional benefits like vision, hearing, or dental coverage. The premiums for these plans can vary, with some costing as low as **$0** in addition to the regular **Part B premium**. For 2024, the average premium is expected to be around **$18.50 per month**, but this figure depends entirely on the specific plan and provider.

Medicare Part D (Prescription Drug Coverage)

Part D plans, which cover prescription drugs, also have varying premiums based on the plan you choose. On average, the monthly premium for Part D is projected to be around **$55.50** in 2024, though this could differ depending on the insurer and the specific benefits offered by the plan.

Understanding Medicare Deductibles

Medicare deductibles refer to the amount you pay out of pocket before Medicare starts to cover a portion of your healthcare costs. Here's a breakdown by part:

Medicare Part A (Hospital Insurance)

The **Part A deductible** for 2024 is **$1,632 per benefit period**. A benefit period begins the day you are admitted to a hospital or skilled nursing facility and ends once you've been out of the hospital or nursing care for 60 consecutive days. This deductible covers your hospital stays, and you won't be responsible for another deductible until a new benefit period begins.

Medicare Part B (Medical Insurance)

For **Part B**, the deductible in 2024 is **$240 per year**. Once this deductible is met, Medicare generally covers 80% of the cost for services like doctor visits and outpatient care, while you cover the remaining 20%.

Medicare Part C and Part D

Since **Medicare Advantage (Part C)** and **Part D** plans are offered through private insurers, deductibles will vary by plan. Some Part C plans may have no deductible at all, while others will have specific deductible amounts for hospital or prescription coverage. For **Part D**, the deductible can be as high as **$545 per year**, though some plans may not require any deductible.

Medicare Copayments and Coinsurance

Medicare operates differently when it comes to copayments and coinsurance, depending on the part of Medicare you're using.

Parts A and B

With **Original Medicare (Parts A and B)**, rather than paying set copayments, you'll be responsible for **coinsurance**, which is a percentage of the costs. For instance, under **Part B**, once your deductible is met, you'll typically pay **20%** of the cost of most services. In **Part A**, coinsurance kicks in after certain thresholds. For example, after 60 days in the hospital, you'll start paying **$408 per day** for your stay.

Medicare Advantage (Part C) and Part D

If you're enrolled in a **Medicare Advantage** or **Part D** plan, you may face copayments for certain services or prescriptions. These copays are predetermined by your plan and could vary depending on the service or drug tier.

Medicare Part A Costs for Hospital and Nursing Care

Medicare Part A primarily covers inpatient hospital care and skilled nursing facility care, but your costs will vary based on how long you need care.

Inpatient Hospital Care

- For the first **60 days** of your hospital stay, Medicare covers the full cost after you pay the deductible of **$1,632** per benefit period.
- From **days 61 to 90**, you'll pay **$408 per day** as coinsurance.
- After **90 days**, you'll pay **$816 per day** for each **lifetime reserve day** (up to 60 days in your lifetime).
- Once you've used all your lifetime reserve days, you'll need to cover all costs.

Skilled Nursing Facility Care

- The first **20 days** of care in a skilled nursing facility are fully covered by Medicare.
- From **days 21 to 100**, you will need to pay **$204 per day**.
- After **day 100**, you are responsible for the full cost of care.

Immunosuppressive Drug Coverage

If you're receiving Medicare benefits due to **end-stage renal disease (ESRD)**, your coverage ends 36 months after a kidney transplant. This means that once this period passes, Medicare will no longer cover the **immunosuppressant drugs** required to prevent your body from rejecting the transplanted organ under **Part B**. However, recognizing the ongoing need for this critical medication, Medicare introduced a new benefit in 2023. This benefit ensures that individuals without other insurance options can continue to afford these life-saving drugs beyond the initial 36-month period. Starting in 2024, the standard monthly fee for this **immunosuppressant drug-only coverage** is **$103**. For individuals with higher incomes, this fee will be tiered, ranging from **$171.70** to **$515.10** per month. It's essential to note that this particular benefit only covers immunosuppressant drugs—other medical services or medications are not included under this new coverage option.

Understanding Medicare Observation Status

Observation status can often be misleading and lead to unexpected costs. When you're admitted to a hospital, you might assume you're an inpatient, but that isn't always the case. In some situations, particularly within the first day or two of your stay, you may be classified under "observation status." This classification means you're considered an outpatient, even though you're physically in the hospital. Being under observation status can be more expensive because Medicare treats this status differently from inpatient care. For example, the coverage and coinsurance rates may be higher for outpatient services, leading to more out-of-pocket expenses for you. To avoid these surprises, it's wise to ask your doctor if you're being treated as an inpatient. If not, you can inquire if it's possible and appropriate to be reclassified as an inpatient to minimize costs.

Medicare Part D (Prescription Drug Coverage) Payments

Enrolling in **Medicare Part D** is crucial if you need prescription drug coverage. Failing to sign up for **Part D** or an equivalent drug plan when you first become eligible may result in a **late enrollment penalty**, which could increase your monthly costs. However, you can avoid this penalty if you already have coverage that Medicare considers comparable, such as through an employer or **TRICARE. There are two primary ways to receive prescription drug coverage:**
1. You can enroll in a **standalone Part D plan** alongside your existing Medicare Parts A or B.
2. Alternatively, you can choose a **Medicare Advantage (Part C)** plan that includes prescription coverage.

If your Part D coverage isn't bundled with your Medicare Advantage plan, you'll need to pay an extra premium for prescription benefits. In 2024, the **average monthly premium** for Part D plans will be approximately **$55.50**, according to estimates from the **Centers for Medicare & Medicaid Services (CMS)**. Keep in mind that if your **2022 tax return** shows a higher income, Medicare will apply an additional charge—ranging from **$12.90** to **$81.00** on top of your regular Part D premium. This additional fee is part of the **Income-Related Monthly Adjustment Amount (IRMAA)**.

Out-of-Pocket Costs in Medicare Part D

After paying your monthly premiums for Part D, there are four key phases of out-of-pocket spending to be aware of:

1. **Deductible Phase**: You must first pay any plan-specific deductible. Not all plans have a deductible, but if they do, this is your initial out-of-pocket cost before the plan starts to share expenses.
2. **Initial Coverage Phase**: After meeting the deductible, you enter the phase where you're responsible for paying a portion of your prescription costs through **copayments** and **coinsurance**.
3. **Coverage Gap (Donut Hole)**: This phase begins once you and your plan have spent **$5,030** on covered medications in 2024. During this period, you will pay no more than **25%** of the cost for your prescription drugs. The gap continues until your total out-of-pocket spending reaches **$8,000**.
4. **Catastrophic Coverage Phase**: Once your out-of-pocket expenses surpass **$8,000**, catastrophic coverage starts. From January 1, 2024, Medicare has eliminated the **5% coinsurance** requirement for this phase, meaning you won't pay anything for your medications for the remainder of the year.

Each January, your coverage resets, returning you to the deductible phase.

New Changes in Medicare Part D

Recent changes have made Medicare Part D more beneficial for those with specific health needs:

- As of **2023**, Medicare has capped the monthly cost of **insulin** at **$35** for covered products, ensuring more predictable expenses for beneficiaries using insulin. This cap may vary slightly if you receive **Extra Help**.
- Additionally, adult vaccines recommended by the **Advisory Committee on Immunization Practices (ACIP)**—including the **shingles vaccine**—are now classified as preventive services under Part D. These vaccines are provided at **no cost**, regardless of whether you've met your plan's deductible.
- Beginning in **2024**, individuals with family incomes up to **150%** of the federal poverty level will qualify for the **Extra Help** subsidy, significantly reducing their out-of-pocket prescription costs.
- By **2025**, Medicare Part D will introduce a **$2,000 annual out-of-pocket limit** on prescription drugs. Furthermore, insurers will be required to offer **payment plans**, allowing enrollees to spread out their out-of-pocket costs over time rather than paying the full amount upfront when picking up prescriptions. This will apply to both standalone **Part D** plans and **Medicare Advantage** plans that include Part D coverage.

Medigap: Covering Out-of-Pocket Costs with a Medicare Supplement Plan:

Original Medicare doesn't have an annual cap on out-of-pocket expenses, meaning that if you require extensive medical care, your costs could add up significantly. Due to this, about half of all Medicare beneficiaries look for extra protection through other sources, such as employer-sponsored insurance, **Medicaid**, or **Medigap** (Medicare Supplement Insurance). These additional options help bridge the gap between what Medicare covers and what you'd otherwise be paying.

Medigap Plans: Extra Protection for Medicare Beneficiaries

Medigap plans, offered by private insurance companies, are designed to follow federal Medicare guidelines, while providing supplementary coverage. These plans vary in terms of the protection they offer, with different levels available depending on the specific Medigap plan you choose. They are named Plans **A**, **B**, **C**, **D**, **F**, **G**, **K**, **L**, **M**, and **N**.

- **Plan F** is considered the most comprehensive of all Medigap plans, but it's only available to those who became eligible for Medicare before January 1, 2020. It covers nearly all out-of-pocket costs not paid by Original Medicare.
- **Plan G** is another highly comprehensive plan, covering almost everything except for the Part B deductible. Plan G remains available to all new Medicare beneficiaries.

Some **Medigap plans** offer an added layer of protection by capping your out-of-pocket spending. Once you hit this threshold, the plan takes over and covers 100% of approved Medicare services for the rest of the year. In 2024, the annual out-of-pocket limits for Medigap plans are **$7,060** for **Plan K** and **$3,530** for **Plan L**.

Medigap Premiums: Variability and Factors to Consider

While the benefits of Medigap plans are standardized by Medicare, the monthly **premiums** for these plans can vary significantly based on factors such as location, insurer, and individual health. For instance, in 2020, the **American Association for Medicare Supplement Insurance** reported that the monthly premium for a **65-year-old woman in Dallas** enrolled in **Plan G** ranged anywhere from **$99 to $381**. These differences in price highlight the importance of comparing plans and premiums before making a decision. When evaluating Medigap options, it's not only important to consider the **premium costs** but also the potential **savings on out-of-pocket expenses**. Some plans with higher premiums might offer more comprehensive coverage, potentially reducing your out-of-pocket expenses to nearly zero. On the other hand, plans with lower premiums may leave you responsible for more costs during the year.

The Importance of Timely Enrollment in Medigap

One of the key benefits of enrolling in **Medigap** when you first become eligible for Medicare is the guarantee of coverage without medical underwriting. If you wait and first enroll in a **Medicare Advantage** plan, and later decide to switch to **Original Medicare** and purchase a Medigap plan, you may face medical underwriting. This process allows insurers to evaluate your health, which can result in higher premiums or even denial of coverage based on your health history.

Is Medicare Advantage a Cheaper Alternative?

For some individuals, **Medicare Advantage (MA)** plans offer a more affordable solution compared to Original Medicare and Medigap. However, it's important to understand the trade-offs that come with this choice. **Medicare Advantage** plans typically have **provider networks**, meaning you're limited to a list of doctors and hospitals that are part of the plan. While this helps keep costs low, it also restricts your freedom to see any doctor you choose, as you can with **Original Medicare**. One of the appealing features of **MA plans** is that they do come with **out-of-pocket limits**, which can offer protection if you require extensive care. In 2024, the average monthly premium for a Medicare Advantage plan is expected to be around **$18.50**, on top of the Part B premium. Many of these plans also bundle **Part D prescription coverage**, although you need to ensure the plan covers the medications you require. If not, you might need to buy a separate **Part D** plan.

Evaluating Medicare Advantage: Potential Pitfalls

While **Medicare Advantage** plans can be a cost-saving option, they may not always be cheaper than **Original Medicare** when you consider all factors. **A study by the Commonwealth Fund highlights some common drawbacks of these plans:**

- **Limited Provider Networks**: You may find that your preferred doctors or specialists are not part of the plan's network.
- **No Medigap Access**: Unlike with Original Medicare, you cannot purchase a **Medigap plan** to help cover additional out-of-pocket expenses if you're enrolled in Medicare Advantage.
- **Risk of Choosing the Wrong Plan**: Many beneficiaries choose their plans based on advertisements rather than their actual health needs, which could lead to unexpected costs.
- **Prior Authorization Requirements**: Some Medicare Advantage plans require prior authorization for specific treatments or procedures. This could lead to delays in receiving care or even denials of coverage, which can be frustrating if you need timely medical services.

Income-Related Monthly Adjustment Amount (IRMAA)

What Is IRMAA?

IRMAA is a monthly fee that is added to your Medicare Part B and D payments depending on how much money you make. Part B includes treatments that are medically necessary or that keep you healthy. What about your regular doctor visits, lab tests, treatments, and even home healthcare? Part B covers all of these things. Part D, on the other hand, covers prescription drugs, so you don't have to pay that much for them. Putting in place the IRMAA method was meant to make the Medicare budget more stable. IRMAA is like a sliding scale: people with higher incomes pay more into Medicare because they can afford it. This helps Medicare stay solvent and ensures everyone gets the care they need. The IRMAA fee is added on the regular premiums for Parts B and D. This is a big part of how much Medicare costs for people with better incomes. This extra cost might make your budget tighter, especially if you are retired. Because of this, learning more about IRMAA and how it is determined can help you better predict how it might affect your finances.

How Is Your IRMAA Calculated?

Many things affect how IRMAA is calculated. Your modified adjusted gross income (MAGI) is the most important of these. To find it, add up your overall adjusted gross income and tax-free interest income. Your IRMAA is also affected by how you file your taxes, such as whether you are single, married filing equally, head of household, or married filing separately. Your IRMAA also takes into account big events in your life that might change your pay, like getting married, divorced, or losing a spouse. The MAGI from your tax return from two years ago is used to figure out your IRMAA. When figuring out your IRMAA for 2024, for example, you will look at your MAGI from 2022. This information is used by the Social Security Administration (SSA) to divide Social Security recipients into groups based on their wealth. An IRMAA fee is added to each of these groups differently. Since there are different income levels, the IRMAA fee will be higher for people in higher-income groups. In turn, IRMAA leads to higher Medicare costs all around. In 2024, for example, people with a MAGI of $206,000 or less won't have to pay an IRMAA. The same goes for married couples with a MAGI of $206,000 or less. Some people, like single people, have to pay extra for IRMAA if they make more than $103,000 a year or $206,000 a year if they are married. This is on top of their regular Part B and Part D payments.

How Much Are IRMAAs and Who Pays Them?

It's important to include the cost of IRMAAs every year in your budget for Medicare costs. If your income is higher than a certain amount, this extra charge is added to your monthly Part B and Part D payments. These costs are on top of your normal Medicare premiums. **Here are the IRMAA rates and income limits for 2024 to give you a better idea:**

2024 Medicare Full Part B: IRMAAs and Total Premiums

MAGI for Beneficiaries Who File Individual Tax Returns	MAGI for Beneficiaries Who File Joint Tax Returns	IRMAA	Total Monthly Premium
Up to $103,000	Up to $206,000	$0.00	$174.70
More than $103,000 and less than or equal to $129,000	More than $206,000 and less than or equal to $258,000	$69.90	$244.60
More than $129,000 and less than or equal to $161,000	More than $258,000 and less than or equal to $322,000	$174.70	$349.40
More than $161,000 and less than or equal to $193,000	More than $322,000 and less than or equal to $386,000	$279.50	$454.20
More than $193,000 and less than $500,000	More than $386,000 and less than $750,000	$384.30	$559.00
More than or equal to $500,000	More than or equal to $750,000	$419.30	$594.00

However, high-income Medicare beneficiaries are subject to different IRMAAs and premiums if they only have Part B immunosuppressive drug coverage:

2024 Medicare Part B Immunosuppressive Drug Coverage Only: IRMAAs and Total Premiums

MAGI for Beneficiaries Who File Individual Tax Returns	MAGI for Beneficiaries Who File Joint Tax Returns	IRMAA	Total Monthly Premium
Up to $103,000	Up to $206,000	$0.00	$103.00
More than $103,000 and less than or equal to $129,000	More than $206,000 and less than or equal to $258,000	$68.70	$171.70
More than $129,000 and less than or equal to $161,000	More than $258,000 and less than or equal to $322,000	$171.70	$274.70
More than $161,000 and less than or equal to $193,000	More than $322,000 and less than or equal to $386,000	$274.70	$377.70
More than $193,000 and less than $500,000	More than $386,000 and less than $750,000	$377.70	$480.70
More than or equal to $500,000	More than or equal to $750,000	$412.10	$515.10

Part D premiums are different for each plan, and the Centers for Medicare and Medicaid Services say that about 8% of recipients pay an IRMAA on top of their premiums. About a third of people pay their premiums and IRMAAs straight to their plan, while the other two-thirds have the money taken out of their Social Security checks.

2024 Medicare Part D IRMAAs

MAGI for Beneficiaries Who File Individual Tax Returns	MAGI for Beneficiaries Who File Joint Tax Returns	IRMAA
Up to $103,000	Up to $206,000	$0.00
More than $103,000 and less than or equal to $129,000	More than $206,000 and less than or equal to $258,000	$12.90
More than $129,000 and less than or equal to $161,000	More than $258,000 and less than or equal to $322,000	$33.30
More than $161,000 and less than or equal to $193,000	More than $322,000 and less than or equal to $386,000	$53.80
More than $193,000 and less than $500,000	More than $386,000 and less than $750,000	$74.20
More than or equal to $500,000	More than or equal to $750,000	$81.00

Appealing Your IRMAA

You can review your IRMAA decision if you don't agree with it or your income has dropped a lot because of life happenings. To file an appeal, you must fill out a form known as SSA-44, which lets you explain why you think the IRMAA decision is wrong and include proof to back up your claims. This could include proof of an event that changed your life or proof that your income has gone down. Once you fill the form, send it to your local Social Security office for review. After that, you will make a new decision based on the information you gave. There are more ways to appeal if you're not happy with the ruling. You can ask for a hearing by an administrative law judge, ask the Appeals Council to look over the case again, or take the case to federal court.

Paying Your IRMAA

How are you going to pay your IRMAA fees? There are several ways to do it. If you get benefits from Social Security or the Railroad Retirement Board, Medicare Part B and IRMAA may be taken out of your payments immediately. If you don't get these benefits, you will get a bill. You can pay it by mail, in person at your local Social Security office, or online through the bill pay service at your bank or Medicare's online Biller Direct Express service. Which payment method is best for you depend on your situation? For instance, if you get monthly benefits, having the costs taken out regularly can make things easier. But, if your income changes often or you'd rather be more in charge of your payments, direct bills might be better for you. Remember that if you're late registering in Part B, you could have to pay a 10% fee for every full 12-month period that your rate is late. This shows how important it is to pay on time. Medicare.gov says that if you sign up for Part D after the deadline, you will have to pay a fine equal to 1% of the national base beneficiary premium times the number of full, uncovered months you didn't have Part D or creditable coverage. So, carefully think about your choices while keeping your spending and living habits in mind.

Bottom Line

Another important part of Medicare is the Income-Related Monthly Adjustment Amount (IRMAA), which makes sure that the healthcare system is fair and stable financially. It changes the premiums for Medicare Parts B and D depending on the beneficiary's income, making those with better incomes pay more. The effects of IRMAA can greatly affect how people plan their budgets, especially when they retire. So, it is very important to know how IRMAA is figured, how much it costs, and how to file an appeal.

CHAPTER 5

MEDICARE AND OTHER HEALTH INSURANCE

How Medicare Works with Employer Insurance

There are a lot of people who work past age 65 or have health insurance through their spouse's job. People who are eligible for Medicare but also have an employer-provided health plan need to know how Medicare works with their employer-provided insurance so they don't have coverage gaps or fines they don't need. How Medicare and employer insurance work together varies on several things, such as the size of the business, the type of coverage, and the person's employment status. **It's important for beneficiaries to know how Medicare works with workplace insurance and what they need to think about when choosing how to handle both types of coverage:**

1. **Employer Size: A Key Factor in Coordination**

One of the most important things that determine how Medicare works with workplace insurance is the size of the business. Depending on the size of the company, Medicare is either the primary payer (the plan that pays first) or the secondary payer (the plan that pays after the main insurance has paid its share).

Medicare and Employer-Sponsored Insurance for Companies with 20 or More Employees

If you or your spouse is employed by a company that has **20 or more employees**, the employer's health insurance will serve as your **primary coverage**, while Medicare will act as the **secondary payer**. In this arrangement, your employer's plan covers your medical bills first. If Medicare also covers the services, it will step in to cover some or all of the remaining costs that your employer plan doesn't pay, which could significantly reduce your out-of-pocket expenses.

Medicare Enrollment for Employees

Many people choose to enroll in **Medicare Part A** when they turn 65, even if they are still receiving health insurance through their employer. This is because Part A, which covers **hospital services**, typically comes at no additional cost if you or your spouse has paid Medicare taxes while working. Even though your employer's plan will likely cover most of your healthcare needs, including prescriptions, enrolling in Part A provides an added layer of protection. However, some individuals opt to **delay enrolling in Medicare Part B**. Since **Part B** comes with a monthly premium and primarily covers outpatient care, such as doctor visits and preventive services, employees may wait to sign up while they are still covered under their employer's plan, especially if their job-based coverage offers sufficient benefits.

Special Enrollment Period (SEP) for Medicare Part B

If you decide to postpone **Part B enrollment** while you are still covered by a large employer plan, you won't face any late enrollment penalties, thanks to a **Special Enrollment Period (SEP)**. This SEP becomes available if you leave your job or lose your employer-sponsored health coverage. Once you're no longer covered by the employer's plan, you'll have **eight months** to enroll in Medicare Part B without incurring any late fees. This period provides ample time to transition into Medicare, ensuring that you maintain continuous healthcare coverage without the risk of higher costs due to delayed registration.

For Employers with Fewer than 20 Employees:

- **Medicare as Primary:** If you or your partner work for a small business with fewer than 20 workers, Medicare usually pays your medical bills when you turn 65, even if you are still on your employer's health insurance plan. The workplace plan is the secondary payer in this case, which means it pays for things like coinsurance, copayments, and deductibles that Medicare doesn't cover.
- **Part B Enrollment:** In this case, it's important to sign up for both Part A and Part B of Medicare when you turn 65, since Medicare will be your main insurance. If you wait too long to sign up for Part B, you might not have enough coverage, and you might be charged extra for enrolling late.
- **Coordination of Benefits:** When Medicare is the main payer, it pays for qualified services first, and if necessary, workplace insurance covers the rest of the costs. For instance, Medicare will pay for 80% of a visit to the doctor, and based on the terms of the plan, the employer's plan may pay for the remaining 20%.

2. **Retiree Health Insurance**

Some companies offer health insurance for retirees, which cover you and your partner even after you leave. **When you're not working, the way benefits are coordinated is different from when you are.**

- **Medicare as Primary:** If you are eligible for Medicare and no longer work, Medicare will pay for your health care. Your retirement health insurance will pay for your care secondarily. In this case, Medicare will pay for medical bills first, and the retirement plan might pay for any costs that are left over, like coinsurance or deductibles.
- **Medigap vs. Retiree Coverage:** Many people choose to add to their Medicare with a Medigap plan instead of using retiree health insurance. It's important to compare features to find the best plan for your needs. Retiree plans might not cover as much as Medigap plans.
- **Prescription Drug Coverage:** Some retiree plans offer prescription drug coverage that may be considered creditable, which means it's at least as good as Medicare Part D. If your retiree plan offers creditable drug coverage, you can wait to sign up for Medicare Part D without having to pay a late enrollment penalty. But if the prescription drug coverage in your retirement plan isn't good enough, you might want to sign up for Part D to avoid fines in the future.

3. **Working Past Age 65: Medicare and COBRA**

COBRA Coverage after Leaving a Job

If you retire or leave your job, you may have the option to keep your employer-sponsored health insurance through **COBRA** (Consolidated Omnibus Budget Reconciliation Act). This program allows you to maintain your health benefits for up to **18 months** after employment ends. **However, it's important to understand how COBRA works with Medicare, especially if you're approaching or over age 65.**

- **How Medicare Works with COBRA:** When you're eligible for both **Medicare** and **COBRA**, **Medicare** generally becomes the **primary payer** for your medical costs, and COBRA acts as the **secondary payer**. This means that Medicare will pay first for covered services, and COBRA will help cover the remaining costs. For example, if you're 65 or older and have both COBRA and Medicare, any medical expenses will be paid by Medicare first, and COBRA will cover what Medicare does not.
- **Key Considerations for COBRA and Medicare:** If you're covered by COBRA and become eligible for **Medicare**, it's usually a smart move to enroll in **Medicare Part B** to ensure you maintain comprehensive coverage. In most cases, once you turn 65, your **COBRA coverage ends** for medical services, although you might be able to continue COBRA for benefits that Medicare doesn't cover, such as **dental** or **vision care**. Be aware that delaying your Medicare Part B enrollment while relying solely on COBRA can lead to a **late enrollment penalty**, which will increase your monthly premiums when you eventually sign up.
- **COBRA and Prescription Drug Coverage (Part D):** If you're receiving prescription drug coverage through COBRA, it's important to find out whether that coverage is considered **creditable**. Creditable coverage means that it's as good as or better than Medicare Part D. If your COBRA prescription coverage isn't considered creditable, you'll need to enroll in **Medicare Part D** when you become eligible, or you may face a **late enrollment penalty**.

4. **Special Enrollment Period (SEP) for Medicare**

If you delay enrolling in **Medicare Part B** because you're still covered by an employer plan, you'll qualify for a **Special Enrollment Period (SEP)** once your workplace coverage ends. This SEP lasts for **eight months** and allows you to sign up for Part B without incurring late fees. **During this period, you can make several key decisions:**

- **Enroll in Medicare Part B**: You can sign up for Part B without paying any penalties, even if you previously delayed enrollment.
- **Choose a Part D Plan**: If your employer's plan didn't include creditable drug coverage, now is the time to enroll in a **Medicare Part D** plan to avoid penalties for late enrollment.
- **Consider Medicare Advantage**: You can opt for a **Medicare Advantage (Part C)** plan, which typically includes coverage for hospital care (Part A), medical services (Part B), and sometimes prescription drugs (Part D).

5. **Dual Coverage: Using Medicare with Employer Insurance**

Some individuals prefer to keep both **Medicare** and their employer-sponsored insurance for added coverage. In this scenario, the two plans work together, with one plan acting as the **primary payer** and the other as the **secondary payer**.

- **Primary and Secondary Payers**: The **primary payer**—whether it's Medicare or your employer's plan—covers the bulk of your medical expenses. The **secondary payer** may cover additional costs, such as copayments, deductibles, or services that the primary payer does not fully cover.
- **Higher Premiums, Broader Coverage**: While having dual coverage means you'll likely need to pay two separate premiums (one for Medicare and one for your employer insurance), it can provide more comprehensive coverage. This setup may help fill in gaps, such as reducing your out-of-pocket expenses for services that aren't fully covered by one plan alone.

6. **Medicare Part D and Employer Prescription Drug Coverage**

If your employer provides prescription drug coverage, it's essential to know whether that coverage is considered **creditable** by Medicare. Creditable coverage ensures that your drug plan is at least as good as **Medicare Part D**. **Depending on whether your employer's coverage is creditable, your options regarding Part D will differ:**

- **If Your Employer Plan Is Creditable**: You don't need to enroll in **Medicare Part D** right away. You can keep your employer's prescription drug plan without worrying about late enrollment penalties.
- **If Your Employer Plan Is Not Creditable**: It's important to enroll in **Medicare Part D** as soon as you're eligible to avoid paying penalties later. If your employer's plan doesn't meet Medicare's standards for prescription drug coverage, delaying your Part D enrollment will lead to higher costs down the road.
- **Notice of Creditable Coverage**: Each year, employers are required to inform you whether or not your prescription drug coverage is creditable. This **Notice of Creditable Coverage** should be kept as proof in case you decide to switch to Medicare Part D later on. Having this documentation can help protect you from any potential penalties if you choose to delay your Part D enrollment.

Retiree Insurance vs. Medicare

There are a lot of complicated rules about health insurance that people have to learn when they go from working to retirement. Two popular types of insurance for retirees are Medicare and retiree insurance from a former job. Even though both choices have important advantages, they work, what they cover, and how much they cost in very different ways. For seniors to make smart choices about their health insurance, they need to know about these changes. Here is a full comparison of Medicare and retirement insurance, including how the two work together, what they cover, and things to think about when choosing which coverage to rely on.

What Is Retiree Insurance?

Some employers offer health insurance to their former workers after they leave. This is called retiree insurance. Medical bills, and sometimes prescription drugs, dental care, and eye care, can be covered by this type of insurance. When an employer offers senior benefits, the coverage is usually the same as it was while the employee was working. **However, some plans may have different terms and prices for retirees.**

- **Eligibility:** Most of the time, retiree insurance is only available to workers who meet certain requirements, like retiring at a certain age or after working for the company for a certain number of years.
- **Coverage for Spouses and Dependents:** Many types of retirement insurance also cover a partner or kids. However once the retiree is qualified for Medicare, the retiree insurance may work differently, usually as extra coverage on top of Medicare.

What Is Medicare?

There is a government health insurance program called Medicare that mostly covers people aged 65 and up, but it also covers younger people with illnesses or certain medical conditions. **Medicare is made up of several parts:**

- **Part A (Hospital Insurance):** Covers inpatient hospital care, skilled nursing facility care, hospice, and some home health services.
- **Part B (Medical Insurance):** Covers outpatient care, doctor visits, preventive services, and durable medical equipment.
- **Part C (Medicare Advantage):** Offers an alternative to Original Medicare, bundling Parts A and B and often including prescription drug coverage and additional benefits like dental and vision.
- **Part D (Prescription Drug Coverage):** Covers prescription medications.

If you've paid Medicare taxes through your job, most people immediately get Medicare when they turn 65. One can use Medicare by itself, or they can add it to other types of insurance, like senior plans.

Coordination of Benefits: Retiree Insurance and Medicare

For most people, Medicare becomes the primary payer when they become eligible for it, and retirement insurance becomes the secondary payer. This means that Medicare will pay for healthcare services first, and then the retirement insurance will pay for some of the rest, like copayments, coinsurance, and deductibles. While some senior plans do work the same way as Medicare, it's important to know how your plan works with Medicare.

Medicare as Primary Coverage

Medicare is usually the main payer for retirees who are eligible for both Medicare and retirement insurance. It pays for it according to its rules, and the gap is made up by pension insurance.

Retiree Insurance as Secondary Coverage

Most of the time, retiree insurance helps pay for things like deductibles, copayments, and coinsurance that Medicare doesn't fully cover. This can cut down on out-of-pocket costs by a lot. What the retirement plan does cover, though, will depend on the insurance policy's terms.

Prescription Drug Coverage

Some retiree plans cover prescription drugs, but not all of them are as good as or better than Medicare Part D. If the retiree plan's drug coverage is creditable, which means it's at least as good as Medicare Part D, retirees may not need to sign up for Part D. If the retiree plan's drug coverage is not creditable, however, retirees should sign up for Medicare Part D to avoid a late enrollment penalty.

Key Differences between Retiree Insurance and Medicare

Coverage Scope

- **Retiree Insurance:** This type of insurance usually covers a lot of different medical services, just like the retiree's insurance did when they were working. It might cover things like dental, eye, and hearing care that aren't covered by Original Medicare. But senior insurance usually has its own rules about what it covers, such as services that aren't covered at all or are limited in some way.
- **Medicare:** Parts A and B of Medicare cover most hospital and medical costs, but there are some services that Medicare doesn't cover, like teeth, vision, hearing aids, and long-term care. The original Medicare plan does not cover these services, but some Medicare Advantage plans may.

Cost Structure

- **Retiree Insurance:** When it comes to retiree insurance, the cost changes a lot depending on the plan and job. People who are retired may have to pay fees, deductibles, copayments, and coinsurance. While some employers may pay some of the fees, retirees may have to pay a bigger portion of the costs than they did when they were working.

- **Medicare:** Part A of Medicare doesn't cost most people anything if they or their partner worked and paid Medicare fees for at least 10 years. Medicare Part B, on the other hand, does have a monthly payment that changes based on your income. Beneficiaries also have to pay coinsurance and fees, which are usually 20% of the amount Medicare approves for Part B treatments. Original Medicare does not have any out-of-pocket limits. However, Medigap or a Medicare Advantage plan can help you handle these costs.

Prescription Drugs

- **Retiree Insurance:** Some insurance plans for retirees cover prescription drugs, but not all do. Retirees should check to see if their prescription drug coverage is comparable to Medicare Part D; if it isn't, they should sign up for Medicare Part D to avoid fines in the future.
- **Medicare Part D:** Part D of Medicare is a separate prescription drug plan that covers most outpatient drugs. There are different Part D plans that beneficiaries can choose from, and each one has its schedule and prices.

Out-of-Pocket Costs

- **Retiree Insurance:** This type of insurance may lower the amount of money you have to pay out of pocket for medical care by paying costs that Medicare doesn't, like copayments and deductibles. However, retirees often have to pay extra for this extra covering, and the amounts can change.
- **Medicare:** People who have Medicare must pay twenty percent of the cost of Part B services, plus any deductibles. They can buy Medigap insurance (Medicare Supplement Insurance) or sign up for a Medicare Advantage plan, which may have out-of-pocket limits if they want extra coverage to lower their out-of-pocket costs.

Access to Providers

- **Retiree Insurance:** Some plans have a provider network, which means that retirees must see certain doctors or hospitals to get the full benefits of the plan. Based on the plan, going out of network could mean higher prices or no service at all.
- **Medicare:** People who have Medicare can see any doctor or hospital that accepts Medicare. This gives them a lot of options. Medicare Advantage plans, on the other hand, might only cover a certain network of doctors, like senior plans.

Pros and Cons of Retiree Insurance

Pros

- **Comprehensive Coverage:** Most of the time, retiree insurance covers more services than Original Medicare does, like dental, eye, and hearing care.
- **Lower Out-of-Pocket Costs:** COBRA and deductibles are two examples of out-of-pocket costs that retirees may have to pay for their health care.
- **Prescription Drug Coverage:** Some plans for retirees cover prescription drugs, which could mean they don't need Medicare Part D.

Cons

- **Premium Costs:** Retirees may have to pay some or all of the premiums for retirement insurance, which can be pricey.
- **Plan Changes:** Employers can change or get rid of retirement benefits at any time, which could mean that retirees have fewer choices or have to pay more.
- **Limited Provider Networks:** Some plans for retirees have limited networks, which mean that retirees may have to switch doctors or pay more for care that isn't covered by the plan.

Pros and Cons of Medicare

Pros

- **Broad Provider Access:** Medicare lets people all over the country choose from many health care providers. Medicare gives beneficiaries more freedom than some retired plans because they can see any doctor or expert who takes Medicare.
- **Cost Predictability:** Medicare payments and cost-sharing amounts are pretty standard, so seniors know exactly how many their monthly costs will be. Medigap and Medicare Advantage plans give you more ways to handle your out-of-pocket costs.

Cons

- **Gaps in Coverage:** Original Medicare doesn't pay for long-term care, dental care, eye care, hearing aids, or vision care, so seniors may need to buy extra coverage to make up for these costs.
- **Out-of-Pocket Costs:** Medicare covers a lot of healthcare costs, but recipients still have to pay their coinsurance and deductibles. With Original Medicare, there is no out-of-pocket cap, but there is additional coverage.

Making the Right Choice: Retiree Insurance, Medicare, or Both?

When choosing whether to use Medicare, senior insurance, or a mix of the two, think about the following:

- **Cost:** Compare the premiums, deductibles, and out-of-pocket costs for both retiree insurance and Medicare. Determine whether the retiree plan's benefits justify the premium costs.
- **Coverage:** Carefully read through each plan to see what it covers, especially when it comes to services like hearing, vision, dental, and prescription drugs. If Medicare doesn't pay for these services, see if your retirement insurance does.
- **Prescription Drug Needs:** You may not need Medicare Part D if your retirement plan covers prescription drugs well enough. If it doesn't, you must sign up for Part D to avoid fines.
- **Provider Access:** Make sure that both Medicare and the senior insurance plan give you access to the doctors and hospitals you want.

COBRA and Medicare: What You Need to Know

People who are looking for health insurance should know about COBRA and Medicare. These are two important choices, especially when things are changing, like when someone retires or changes jobs. The Consolidated Omnibus Budget Reconciliation Act, or COBRA, lets people keep their employer-provided health insurance for a short time after they lose their job. In contrast, Medicare is a government health insurance program that mostly helps people 65 and older, but it also helps some younger people with disabilities. To make sure you always have health insurance and avoid making mistakes that cost a lot of money, you need to know how these two programs work together. Below is an in-depth explanation of how COBRA and Medicare work together, what individuals need to consider, and how to avoid penalties or gaps in coverage.

What is COBRA?

COBRA lets workers and their families keep using their employer-provided health insurance plan for a certain amount of time after they lose their job, have their hours cut, or go through other qualified life events. This extra coverage usually lasts for up to 18 months, but in some cases, like when someone gets sick or divorced, COBRA coverage can last for up to 36 months. But, COBRA can be pricey because the person generally pays the whole premium plus a 2% administrative fee, meaning that you'll pay both the employer and employee parts of the premium.

What is Medicare?

Medicare is a federal health insurance program primarily designed to provide coverage for individuals aged **65 and older**, although it also extends to younger individuals with certain disabilities or health conditions. Medicare is divided into several key parts, each covering different aspects of healthcare.

Parts of Medicare

- **Part A (Hospital Insurance):** This portion of Medicare covers the cost of **inpatient hospital care**, stays in **skilled nursing facilities, hospice care**, and certain forms of **home health services**. Most beneficiaries do not pay a premium for Part A if they or their spouse have paid Medicare taxes during their working years.
- **Part B (Medical Insurance): Part B** provides coverage for **outpatient services**, such as **doctor visits**, preventive care like screenings and vaccines, and the use of **durable medical equipment** (e.g., walkers, wheelchairs). Unlike Part A, Part B generally requires a monthly premium.
- **Part C (Medicare Advantage): Medicare Advantage** plans offer an all-in-one alternative to Original Medicare. These plans are provided by private insurers and typically bundle **Part A, Part B**, and sometimes **Part D** coverage. In addition to hospital and medical care, many Medicare Advantage plans offer extra benefits, such as **vision, dental**, or **hearing coverage**.
- **Part D (Prescription Drug Coverage): Part D** is the portion of Medicare that covers **prescription medications**. It is offered by private insurance companies and can be added to Original Medicare (Parts A and B) or included as part of a Medicare Advantage plan.

When Can You Enroll in Medicare?

Most people become eligible for Medicare at age **65**, and it's crucial to sign up during the **Initial Enrollment Period (IEP)** to avoid late enrollment penalties. The IEP lasts for **seven months**, starting **three months before** your 65th birthday, includes the **month of your birthday**, and extends for **three months after**. During this time, you can enroll in **Part A, Part B**, or both, depending on your healthcare needs. For those who miss their IEP, there may be other opportunities to enroll, but these often come with late enrollment penalties or restricted coverage options until the next **General Enrollment Period** or **Special Enrollment Period**.

How COBRA and Medicare Work Together

Navigating the relationship between **COBRA** and **Medicare** can be complicated, particularly if you have COBRA first and then become eligible for Medicare, or if you already have Medicare and then become eligible for COBRA. Understanding how these programs interact is key to making informed coverage choices and avoiding unnecessary costs.

Scenario 1: If You Have COBRA First and Then Become Eligible for Medicare

If you're enrolled in **COBRA** and later become eligible for **Medicare**, your COBRA coverage will most likely end. According to COBRA rules, individuals can lose their continued COBRA benefits once they qualify for Medicare. The exact timing of this change depends on the terms of your COBRA plan. For example, if you sign up for **Medicare Part A** or **Part B** while still on COBRA, your employer could terminate your COBRA coverage. However, your **spouse** or **dependents** may still be able to keep their COBRA benefits for the remainder of the eligible period. Even if you're covered under COBRA, it's vital to enroll in **Medicare Part B** as soon as you become eligible. At that point, **Medicare becomes your primary insurance**, and COBRA serves as secondary, offering additional coverage for costs Medicare doesn't cover. Failing to enroll in Part B by your eligibility date could leave you without coverage for outpatient services, and you may also face a **late enrollment penalty** when you do sign up for Part B. For example, if you're **65 years old** and still on COBRA but delay enrolling in **Medicare Part B** thinking COBRA will cover all your needs, you could face a major issue down the road. If you need outpatient care, Medicare won't pay for it since you missed the initial sign-up period, and COBRA will only act as secondary insurance. Since COBRA expects Medicare to be the primary payer, you could end up being responsible for the entire bill, which can be a costly mistake.

Scenario 2: If You Have Medicare First and Then Become Eligible for COBRA

If you already have **Medicare** and then qualify for **COBRA**, such as after losing your job or reducing your work hours, you can still elect to receive COBRA coverage. However, COBRA will serve as **supplemental insurance** to Medicare; meaning that **Medicare will pay first** for your medical services, and COBRA can help cover additional costs like **copayments**, **deductibles**, or **coinsurance**. To make the most of COBRA coverage, it's crucial that you're already enrolled in **Medicare Part B**. Without Part B, COBRA won't pay for services that Part B would have covered. For instance, if you only have **Medicare Part A** and delay enrolling in Part B because you have COBRA, you could end up paying large out-of-pocket costs for outpatient care since COBRA won't cover what Medicare Part B normally would. One advantage of COBRA in this situation is that it may cover services Medicare doesn't, such as **dental**, **vision**, or **prescription drugs** (if you haven't enrolled in **Medicare Part D**). However, COBRA tends to be expensive, so it's a good idea to compare the cost and benefits of COBRA with a **Medigap** or **Medicare Advantage** plan, both of which might provide similar coverage at a lower cost.

Enrollment Timing: Avoiding Penalties and Gaps in Coverage

When it comes to enrolling in Medicare or COBRA, timing is crucial to ensure you maintain coverage and avoid late enrollment penalties. Here are a few key situations to consider:

- **If you're 65 or Older and Become Eligible for Medicare While on COBRA**: You should sign up for **Medicare Parts A and B** as soon as you become eligible. Delaying **Part B** enrollment could lead to a **late enrollment penalty**, meaning you may pay higher premiums for the rest of your life. Additionally, if you don't sign up during the **Initial Enrollment Period (IEP)**, you may have to wait until the **General Enrollment Period (GEP)** (January 1 to March 31 each year), and your coverage won't begin until **July 1**.
- **If You Become Eligible for COBRA After Enrolling in Medicare**: You can still sign up for COBRA to supplement your **Medicare** coverage. In this case, **Medicare pays first**, and COBRA helps cover any remaining costs. COBRA can also cover services that Medicare doesn't, such as **dental** or **vision care**, depending on the specifics of your COBRA plan.
- **If You Delay Medicare Enrollment Because of COBRA**: It's important to know that COBRA does not count as a reason to delay enrolling in **Medicare Part B**. If you wait to sign up for Medicare until COBRA ends, you could face penalties and gaps in coverage. For this reason, it's best to enroll in Medicare when you're first eligible, even if you have COBRA.

Costs of COBRA vs. Medicare

One of the main reasons people hesitate to drop COBRA when they become eligible for **Medicare** is the perceived cost savings. However, COBRA can actually be quite expensive since you're typically responsible for paying the **full premium**—including both the employer and employee portions—plus an additional **2% administrative fee**. This means COBRA could cost significantly more than a combination of **Medicare** and supplemental coverage. Most people don't pay anything for **Medicare Part A**, but **Part B** does come with a monthly premium, which can vary based on income. Adding a **Medicare Advantage** or **Medigap** plan often results in a total cost that is lower than COBRA premiums. For example, **Medicare Advantage plans** frequently offer additional benefits like **dental**, **vision**, and **prescription drug coverage**, potentially making COBRA unnecessary. **Medigap plans** are designed to cover the out-of-pocket expenses that Medicare leaves behind, like deductibles and coinsurance, providing even more financial protection.

Prescription Drug Coverage and COBRA

If you currently have **prescription drug coverage** through your **COBRA** plan, it may be possible to retain that coverage after transitioning to **Medicare**. However, it's crucial to verify whether your COBRA drug plan qualifies as **creditable coverage**. Creditable coverage means that the prescription benefits provided by your COBRA plan are at least as comprehensive as what

Medicare Part D offers. If your COBRA plan's drug coverage is deemed creditable, you can delay enrolling in **Medicare Part D** without facing any penalties for late enrollment. This gives you the flexibility to continue using your COBRA prescription coverage for as long as it's available. However, if your COBRA drug coverage is **not creditable**, you should enroll in **Medicare Part D** as soon as you're eligible to avoid any future **late enrollment penalties**. If your COBRA drug coverage isn't creditable, you should sign up for Medicare Part D as soon as you can to avoid having to pay a charge. With this plan, you could keep COBRA for other health care costs and switch to Medicare Part D for your drugs. To make sure you keep your health insurance and avoid extra costs or fines, you need to know how COBRA and Medicare work together. Whether COBRA is your first insurance before switching to Medicare or you're already on Medicare and are thinking about adding COBRA as an addition, it's important to make smart choices about when to join and what kind of coverage you need. Remember that once you become eligible, Medicare will usually pay for most of your costs. If you wait to sign up for Medicare Part B and only use COBRA, you could lose coverage and possibly have to pay fines. Carefully weigh the costs and advantages of COBRA and Medicare to pick the plan that best fits your needs as you move toward retirement or when your job situation changes.

Coordination with Veterans' Benefits and TRICARE

If you are qualified for both Medicare and Veterans' Benefits or TRICARE (health insurance for military members, retired, and their families), you need to know how these programs work together to get the most out of your healthcare benefits. Medicare and these health care services for military members offer good coverage, but they don't always work together. Beneficiaries can get the most out of their benefits and avoid having to pay extra costs if they know the rules about coordination. **Here is a detailed account of how Medicare works with Veterans' Benefits and TRICARE, including important things to keep in mind if you have more than one health insurance plan:**

1. **Medicare and Veterans' Benefits**

The Department of Veterans Affairs (VA) handles Veterans' Benefits, which are health care benefits for veterans who qualify based on their service experience, disability status, income, and placement in a priority group. If you are eligible for both Medicare and Veterans' Benefits, they will not work together or organize your funds; you have to pick which app to use when you need care instead.

Key Points about Medicare and Veterans' Benefits Coordination

- **Separate Systems:** Medicare and VA health benefits are two different systems. Medicare won't pay anything if you get care at a VA hospital, instead your VA benefits will cater for it. If you get care at a hospital that isn't run by the VA, on the other hand, Medicare will pay for the services (as long as they are Medicare-approved), but VA benefits won't apply.
- **Use of VA Facilities:** VA health care only pays for care that is given at VA hospitals or facilities approved by the VA. You might not need Medicare for certain services if you

decide to get all of your care at VA parks. Still, Medicare is important if you ever need to get care from somewhere other than the VA.

- **Using Medicare Outside the VA System:** When you use Medicare outside of the VA system, Medicare will pay for your care at a hospital or with a provider that is not part of the VA system, as long as the services are Medicare-approved. This is especially important if you need care right away or if you live far away from a VA hospital and would rather use local doctors.
- **Medicare and VA Enrollment:** For the most options, many soldiers choose to sign up for both Medicare and the VA. In this way, you can get medical care from both VA centers and private hospitals and doctors. This makes sure that you are covered for a bigger range of medical scenarios, such as emergencies that might happen when you are not near a VA center.
- **Prescription Drug Coverage:** One of the benefits of being a VA member is that VA shops cover prescription drugs, and the prices are often lower than Medicare Part D plans. Veterans who get their medicines from the VA may not need to sign up for a Medicare Part D plan, but it's still a good idea to make sure you're covered for meds if you go to a doctor outside of the VA system. Some soldiers sign up for a cheap Part D plan just to make sure they are covered when they are not at a VA facility.

Pros and Cons of Using Medicare and VA Together

Pros

- **Flexibility:** Veterans can pick between using VA healthcare for some services and Medicare for others, based on their medical needs, where they live, and how convenient it is for them.
- **Emergency Coverage:** If you can't get to a VA hospital, Medicare can pay for emergency care.
- **Broader Network:** Medicare lets you see doctors and experts who are not part of the VA system who are civilians.

Cons

- **Separate Billing Systems:** You can't pay for the same service with VA benefits and Medicare. When you need help, you'll have to pick which tool to use.
- **Potentially Redundant Coverage:** Some veterans may not use Medicare much if they get a lot of care from the VA, but it's still a good idea to have Medicare for care that isn't provided by the VA.

2. **Medicare and TRICARE**

The health care program for active-duty and retired military troops, their families, and orphans is called TRICARE. It has many plans, such as TRICARE Prime, TRICARE Select, and TRICARE for

Life (TFL). For people who are qualified for both Medicare and TRICARE, these two programs can work together to cover all of your medical needs.

Key Points about Medicare and TRICARE Coordination

TRICARE for Life (TFL): This is the program that is meant to work with Medicare. If you want to keep getting TRICARE benefits after you become eligible for Medicare (usually at age 65), you have to sign up for both Medicare Part A and Part B. **Medicare would be the main payer in this case, and TRICARE for Life would be the backup payer.**

- If you get a service that is accepted by Medicare, Medicare will pay part of the cost. TRICARE for Life will then pay the rest, which includes copayments, coinsurance, and deductibles. When you use both programs together, you don't have to pay for most of the services that are provided.
- TRICARE for Life may still cover some services that Medicare doesn't, like some dental work or care given abroad. It depends on the service and where it's given, though.

TRICARE and Medicare Parts A & B: If you are eligible for Medicare and want to keep your TRICARE benefits, you must sign up for Medicare Parts A and B. If you don't, you could lose your TRICARE for Life coverage. If you've worked long enough or through your spouse's job, you won't have to pay the Part A premium, but you will have to pay the Part B premium. TRICARE for Life, on the other hand, often makes up for this by offering more complete coverage and lower out-of-pocket costs.

TRICARE and Medicare Advantage (Part C): When you sign up for TRICARE or Medicare Advantage (Part C), you can choose to join a Medicare Advantage plan instead of Original Medicare. If you have TRICARE, on the other hand, you might not need or want a Medicare Advantage plan because TRICARE for Life already covers things that Medicare doesn't fully cover. Signing up for a Medicare Advantage plan could make coordinating benefits harder, and people who already have Medicare may not see the point of it.

Prescription Drug Coverage: If you have TRICARE for Life, you don't need to sign up for a Medicare Part D prescription drug plan. Through TRICARE Pharmacy, TRICARE's drug coverage is called creditable, which means it meets or beats the requirements of Medicare Part D. This makes sure that you are covered for all of your prescription drugs without having to sign up for a different Part D plan.

How TRICARE for Life and Medicare Work Together

- **For Medicare-Covered Services:** Medicare will pay first for any services covered by Medicare. Then, TRICARE for Life will pay the rest of the cost. Most of the time, this means you won't have to pay anything extra for things that Medicare covers.
- **For Services Not Covered by Medicare:** TRICARE for Life may pay for some services that Medicare doesn't like care given outside of the U.S. TRICARE covers medical care abroad, which makes it very useful for retired people who live or visit abroad.

- **Overseas Care:** Medicare doesn't usually pay for medical care outside of the U.S., but TRICARE for Life does. TRICARE for Life will pay for your medical care if you need it while living or visiting abroad.
- **Out-of-Pocket Costs:** People who get Medicare and TRICARE together usually have very little out-of-pocket costs. Cost-sharing amounts for Medicare, like deductibles and coinsurance, are covered by TRICARE for Life. This means that when the two programs work together, most services are fully covered.

Pros and Cons of Using TRICARE and Medicare Together

Pros

- **Comprehensive Coverage:** Medicare and TRICARE for Life together provide very complete coverage, with TRICARE paying for most of the costs that Medicare doesn't.
- **Minimal Out-of-Pocket Costs:** Because TRICARE for Life pays for some medical care, recipients usually don't have to pay much out of pocket for these services.
- **Overseas Care:** TRICARE for Life covers care that is given outside of the U.S. This is a big benefit for people who live or move outside U.S.
- **Prescription Drug Coverage:** TRICARE's drugstore benefits cover all prescription drugs, so you don't need a separate Medicare Part D plan.

Cons

- **Medicare Part B Premium:** Beneficiaries have to pay the Medicare Part B payment, which can be hard for some people, especially retirees with higher incomes.
- **Redundant Medicare Advantage Plans:** It might not be worth the money to sign up for Medicare Advantage plans if TRICARE for Life already covers everything.

3. **Deciding Between Veterans' Benefits, TRICARE, and Medicare**

For people who are qualified for Medicare, Veterans' Benefits, and TRICARE, it's important to know how the different programs work together and when to use each one.

For Veterans with VA Benefits Only: Veterans with VA benefits can only use VA healthcare for certain services. They can use Medicare for care at private hospitals or when VA facilities are not handy. Medicare can also help people get to more experts and therapists outside of the VA system.

For Veterans with Both VA Benefits and TRICARE: Some types of care can be provided by the VA system for veterans who also have TRICARE for Life. Other types of care can be provided by TRICARE for veterans who are serving in combat or for services that are not covered by Medicare. For general private healthcare, veterans can use Medicare. This gives you the most options and covers everything.

CHAPTER 6
MEDIGAP (MEDICARE SUPPLEMENT INSURANCE)

What is Medigap and How Does It Work?

Medigap, often referred to as Medicare Supplement Insurance, is a sort of private health insurance that assists in covering some of the out-of-pocket expenses that are not fully covered by Original Medicare (Part A and Part B). These expenses may include copayments, coinsurance, and deductibles, all of which have the potential to accumulate over time, particularly if you require extensive medical treatment regularly. Medigap is intended to supplement Original Medicare by filling in the gaps that are left by Medicare coverage, offering beneficiaries financial security, and assisting them in managing the expenses of their healthcare responsibilities.

What is Medigap?

Individuals who are enrolled in Original Medicare (Parts A and B) are eligible to purchase Medigap, which is a supplemental insurance coverage distributed by private insurance firms. The amount of money that recipients are required to pay out of pocket is reduced as a result of this assistance in covering healthcare expenditures that Medicare does not pay for. When it comes to Medigap plans, federal and state regulations are responsible for standardizing and regulating them; meaning that any plan that has the same letter (for example, Plan G) provides the same benefits, regardless of which insurance company sells it. Plan A, Plan B, Plan G, Plan N, and so on are some of the numerous plan letters that are used to identify the various Medigap plans that are available. Each of these plan letters provides a different level of coverage. Therefore, Plan G from one insurer will provide the same benefits as Plan G from another insurer, even though the premiums may be different. This is because these plans are identical throughout the majority of states.

How Medigap Works with Medicare

In addition to Original Medicare, Medigap plans are also available. First, Medicare will pay for its portion of the expenses associated with the healthcare services that you get. After that, your Medigap policy will kick in to cover part or all of the remaining costs, depending on the plan that you have. **This cooperation involves the following steps:**
- **Medicare Pays First:** When you get medical care, Medicare Part A (hospital insurance) and Medicare Part B (medical insurance) will pay their respective portions of the cost. This is the first step in the Medicare payment process. Typically, Medicare will pay eighty percent of the authorized amount for Part B services. This means that you will be

responsible for paying the remaining twenty percent of the coinsurance, in addition to any deductibles and copayments that may be applicable.
- **Medigap Pays Second:** Following the payment of Medicare's portion of the out-of-pocket expenses, your Medigap coverage will assist in covering the remaining costs that are incurred by you. For instance, if you have a Medigap plan that covers the coinsurance for Part B, then your policy will pay the remaining twenty percent of the expenditures that Medicare did not cover.

Plans that are part of Medicare Advantage (Part C) are not compatible with Medigap coverage. The sole purpose they serve is to augment the original Medicare program. If you decide to enroll in a Medicare Advantage plan, you will not be able to get Medigap insurance to cover the out-of-pocket expenses that are associated with the Medicare Advantage plan.

Standardized Medigap Plans

As was indicated before, Medigap plans are standardized and are denoted by one of many letters. Different plans provide varying degrees of coverage, and some plans cover a greater proportion of the patient's out-of-pocket expenses than others. **Listed below is a breakdown of the most prevalent Medigap plans by type:**
- **Plan A:** This plan provides coverage for the fundamental benefits that are necessary for all Medigap plans. These benefits include hospital fees and coinsurance for Part A, as well as coinsurance for Part B and the first three pints of blood.
- **Plan B:** Coverage for the Part A deductible is included in Plan B, in addition to everything else that is included in Plan A.
- **Plan D:** Offers coverage that is more complete, covering the basic benefits and the deductibles for Part A, but it does not cover the deductible for Part B or the excess charges.
- **Plan G:** Plan G is easily one of the most well-known and all-encompassing Medigap Insurance Plans. Except for the Medicare Part B deductible, it covers almost all of the expenditures that are incurred out of pocket. Beneficiaries who desire maximum coverage with low out-of-pocket payments frequently go for Plan G as their health insurance plan of choice.
- **Plans K and L:** These plans have cheaper premiums, but they only cover a percentage of the cost-sharing that Medicare requires (for example, around fifty percent or seventy-five percent of expenditures, depending on the plan). Both have a yearly out-of-pocket maximum, beyond which they are responsible for paying the full amount of those services that are covered for the balance of the year.
- **Plan N:** Plan N is a plan that covers the majority of out-of-pocket expenses; nevertheless, beneficiaries may be required to make copayments for visits to the doctor and trips to the emergency department. In return for cheaper premiums, it is a more cost-effective choice for those who are ready to spend a comparatively small amount out of their own money.
- **Plans C and F:** Individuals who become eligible for Medicare after January 1, 2020, are no longer eligible to enroll in Plans C and F. These plans are no longer accessible.

Despite this, those persons who were qualified before this date are still able to acquire them. The Medicare Part B deductible is included in Plan F, which is the most comprehensive plan available. It covers all out-of-pocket payments that are approved by Medicare.

What Medigap Does Not Cover

Even though Medigap can offer considerable financial security by covering the majority of out-of-pocket expenses incurred by Original Medicare recipients, it does not always cover everything. **In general, Medigap insurance does not cover the following:**

- **Prescription Drugs:** Because Medigap plans do not include coverage for prescription drugs, policyholders need to enroll in a separate Medicare Part D plan to have their prescriptions covered.
- **Long-Term Care:** Custodial care in a nursing home or prolonged in-home care are examples of long-term care services that are not covered by Medigap (Medicare Supplement Insurance).
- **Dental, Vision, or Hearing Services:** The Medigap insurance plan does not cover routine dentistry, vision, or hearing care services. This includes examinations, eyeglasses, and hearing aids. Routine dental, vision, and hearing care services are not covered.
- **Private-Duty Nursing or Non-Medicare Services:** Generally speaking, Medigap does not cover services that are not approved by Medicare, such as private-duty nursing or services that are not covered by Medicare.

When it comes to beneficiaries who require coverage for prescription pharmaceuticals, long-term care, dental and vision treatments, or other services, it may be required to purchase supplementary insurance plans to address the gaps in coverage.

Medigap Premiums and Costs

The price of a Medigap policy might change depending on several different factors, including the following:

- **The Plan Letter:** The premium will be greater if the plan is more thorough. Plan G, for instance, is typically more expensive than Plan A or Plan N because it pays for almost all of the participant's out-of-pocket expenses.
- **Insurance Provider:** Even though Medigap plans are standardized, private insurance firms are responsible for determining their prices. Since this is the case, various insurers may offer you different costs for the same plan (for example, Plan G).
- **Geographic Location:** The prices for Medigap insurance might change depending on where you're located. Certain regions have greater healthcare expenditures, which might cause premiums to increase.
- **Age and Health:** In many states, insurers can base your Medigap rates on either your age (also known as an attained-age rating) or your health at the time of purchase (if you apply for Medigap coverage outside of your Medigap Open Enrollment Period).

In general, Medigap plans are more expensive than Medicare Advantage plans; nevertheless, they provide more predictable expenses. When they require medical attention, individuals who have a Medigap plan often do not have to be concerned about the large out-of-pocket payments that they would incur.

Enrolling in Medigap

It is recommended that you purchase Medigap coverage during your Medigap Open Enrollment Period, which begins the first month that you are 65 years old or older and enrolled in Medicare Part B. **This period lasts for a total of six months and includes the following categories:**

- **Guaranteed Issue Rights:** If you have a pre-existing health condition, insurance companies are prevented from denying you coverage or charging you additional charges. This is because you have guaranteed issue rights.
- **No Medical Underwriting:** During your Open Enrollment Period, you are not subject to medical underwriting. This means that the insurance company cannot base its decision on your premium or coverage on your current state of health.

If you attempt to enroll in Medigap outside of your Open Enrollment Period, insurance companies may employ medical underwriting to determine whether or not to accept your application and whether or not to charge you extra rates, depending on the medical condition of the recipient.

Switching Medigap Plans

In most states, you can switch **Medigap** (Medicare Supplement) plans at any time during the year. However, if you're not eligible for a **special enrollment period**, you may be subject to **medical underwriting**. This means that the insurance company could review your health history before deciding whether to offer coverage or set your premiums. If you have **guaranteed issue rights**, insurance companies cannot deny you coverage or increase your premiums based on your health status. These rights usually apply in specific circumstances, such as if you lose your other health insurance, move out of your plan's service area, or if your `goes out of business. Additionally, if you relocate outside of your plan's coverage area, you may also qualify for guaranteed issue rights. However, it's important to understand that switching Medigap plans after your **Open Enrollment Period** can be more challenging, especially if you have **pre-existing conditions**. Outside of the **guaranteed issue periods**, insurers are allowed to use medical underwriting, meaning they may raise your premiums or deny coverage based on your health status.

Medigap vs. Medicare Advantage

There are a lot of people who are faced with the decision of whether to enroll in a Medicare Advantage plan or a Medigap plan. **These are some of the most important distinctions:**

- **Medigap** is intended to be a supplement to Original Medicare, covering the out-of-pocket expenses that Medicare does not pay for. You can visit any physician or facility that is willing to take Medicare as payment. The monthly premiums for Medigap policies are higher, but they can give more predictable expenses since, in most cases, you won't be required to make copayments or pay much higher coinsurance rates.

- **Medicare Advantage (Part C)** is an alternative to Original Medicare that combines hospital, medical, and frequently prescription drug coverage into a single plan. Additionally, Medicare Advantage plans often come with copayments, coinsurance, and networks of physicians and hospitals, but Medigap policies typically have premiums that are cheaper than Medicare Advantage plans. When it comes to seeing experts, you might also need to seek references.

Choosing the Right Medigap Plan

The plan that is best for you is determined by your individual preferences as well as the amount of medical treatment that you anticipate needing during that particular year. The plans provide a variety of advantages, with some of them paying a significant portion of your Medicare expenses while others ask you to share a greater portion of those expenses. **Plans C and F**. Plan F has always been the most popular option due to the extensive benefits it offers. Medicare Part A hospital deductible and co-payments, Medicare Part B deductible, and some emergency care services provided outside of the United States are all covered under this plan. Although Plan C provides coverage for many of the same benefits as Plan F, it does not pay for the excess payment that is associated with Part B. This occurs when a provider requests payment from Medicare that is more than the amount that has been authorized by the program. Thereafter, the recipient is the one who is accountable for the surplus amount. Plans C and F, on the other hand, are no longer accessible to anyone who obtained Medicare eligibility after the first of the year 2020. Plans that provide Medigap coverage are no longer permitted to pay for Part B deductibles. Because both of these plans covered that expense, insurance providers are no longer able to provide additional beneficiaries with them. Those individuals who are already enrolled in those plans are permitted to maintain their insurance coverage. However, because these plans are no longer able to absorb new subscribers, it is anticipated that rates will increase.

Plan G offers coverage that is identical to that of Plan F, except for the Part B deductible. If you were thinking about purchasing Plan F, you should switch to Plan G instead. **Plan G**. As a result of the discontinuation of the well-liked Medigap Plan F, Plan G has emerged as the preferred option for a few individuals. Plan F is widely regarded as the most comprehensive Medigap policy available, while Plan G is the only one that comes extremely close to matching the coverage provided by Plan F. Plan G does not pay the Part B deductible, which goes up to $240 in 2024. This is the most notable difference between the two plans. In the same way that Medigap Plan F pays excess charges, Plan G also covers excess charges. This means that hospitals that do not accept the full amount that Medicare has approved as full payment can charge you up to fifteen percent more than the amount that Medicare has allowed for services or procedures. Several states have prohibited the use of excess charges, including Connecticut, Massachusetts, Minnesota, New York, Ohio, Pennsylvania, Rhode Island, and Vermont.

Plan D. Plan D is comparable to Plan G in that it provides coverage that exceeds that of the majority of Medigap plans; but, in contrast to Plan G, it does not pay any excess expenses. **Plan M**. Although Plan D pays the entire Medicare Part A deductible, Plan M only covers half of it. Plan M is essentially identical to Plan D, however, Plan D covers the entire deductible. **Plans K and L.** Plan K and Plan L of the Medicare Supplement Insurance Program are more affordable than other Medigap insurance. Because you will also be responsible for sharing the cost of coinsurance for your Plan K and L bills (that is, fifty percent for K and twenty-five percent for L) up to an annual out-of-pocket maximum, these two plans have a lower monthly basis. Your cost-sharing arrangement will come to an end whenever you exceed the yearly out-of-pocket maximum for Plan K or Plan L. For Medigap plans K and L, the out-of-pocket (OOP) limitations for the year 2024 are $7,060 and $3,530, respectively. Plan N is an option to consider if you do not anticipate having a significant number of trips to the doctor. This plan often offers reduced rates in exchange for some cost-sharing. **Plan N.** Plan N is the third most prevalent form of Medigap plan, and it is responsible for insuring around 10% of all Medigap members. Plan N features premiums that are cheaper than those of other popular alternatives such as Plan G and Plan F. Plan N pays every one of the costs associated with Part B treatments, except copayments for some office visits and certain trips to the emergency department.

Following the completion of the Part B deductible, the copayments for Plan N visits can reach up to $20 for visits to the doctor and up to $50 for trips to the emergency department in 2024. In addition, the Part A deductible, which is valued at $1,632 in 2024, is covered by Plan N. There is no coverage for Part B excess costs under Plan N. **Plans A and B**. If you desire additional coverage than Medicare Parts A and B but don't anticipate the need for a significant number of medical services, Plan A is the best option for you. Plan A is comprised of simply the fundamentals of Medigap plans, which are the benefits that are covered by every Medigap plan. Plan B offers the same advantages as Plan A, with the additional benefit of paying the Part A deductible, which gives a slightly higher level of coverage for hospitalization. The premiums for Plans A and B are lower, and although you won't be required to pay for additional coverage that you might not use, you might be responsible for any out-of-pocket expenses that may arise. **High deductible plans**. There is the possibility of selling Medigap Plans F and G with a high deductible alternative. Those individuals who are not new to Medicare before January 1, 2020, are the only ones who are eligible to purchase the high-deductible version of Plan F. Individuals who are new to Medicare on or after January 1, 2020, are eligible to enroll in a health insurance plan with a high deductible. For some time before June 1, 2010, Medigap Plan J was also available for purchase with a high deductible. When 2024 rolls around, the yearly deductible cost for these three plans is going to be $2,800. The amount of the deductible for the high-deductible version of plans G, F, and J shows the yearly out-of-pocket expenditures (excluding premiums) that you are required to pay before your coverage begins to take effect.

The Best Time to Enroll in Medigap

Knowing when to enroll in **Medigap** (Medicare Supplement Insurance) is key to ensuring that you get the best coverage at the most affordable rate. **Medigap plans** help cover out-of-pocket costs that **Original Medicare** doesn't, such as **copayments**, **coinsurance**, and **deductibles**. By enrolling at the right time, you can avoid higher premiums due to health conditions and secure **guaranteed coverage** without the risk of denial. The ideal time to sign up for Medigap is during your **Medigap Open Enrollment Period**. This period begins when you are both **65 years old** and enrolled in **Medicare Part B**. It lasts for six months and guarantees that you can enroll in any Medigap plan available in your area without medical underwriting. This means insurers cannot charge you higher rates or deny you coverage based on your health status during this period. Failing to enroll during this time could result in higher premiums or even denial of coverage if you have pre-existing conditions, as insurers may require **medical underwriting** outside the **Open Enrollment Period**.

The Medigap Open Enrollment Period

You should enroll in Medigap during your Medigap Open Enrollment Period since this is the optimum time to do so. The month when you reach 65 and are enrolled in Medicare Part B marks the beginning of this one-time window that lasts for six months. **This window is significant because it is during this time that you have assured issue rights, which means that:**

- **No Medical Underwriting:** There is no medical underwriting, which means that insurance firms are not allowed to refuse you coverage or charge you extra rates because of your current health status or medical illnesses that you have had in the past.
- **Full Coverage:** Your Medigap plan will cover your healthcare costs immediately, even if you have pre-existing conditions. However, some plans may impose a waiting period of six months before covering costs related to pre-existing conditions; however, this waiting period can be waived if you had creditable coverage before enrolling in the plan.

During this period of six months, you have the opportunity to enroll in any Medigap insurance that is offered in your state. Insurers are obligated to sell you coverage at the regular rate for your age, regardless of whether or not your health is a factor.

Why Enrolling during This Period is Important

If you do not enroll in Medigap during the Open Enrollment Period, insurance providers may ask you to undergo medical underwriting when you seek coverage in the future. Given this information, they may refuse to provide coverage, increase your rates, or eliminate coverage for certain pre-existing diseases. Further enrollment chances may be available in some states; however, these opportunities often come with fewer safeguards than the original enrollment period.

Special Enrollment Rights (Guaranteed Issue Rights)

After the Medigap Open Enrollment Period has ended, there are some circumstances in which you can be eligible for guaranteed issue rights, which would allow you to acquire Medigap insurance without having to undergo medical underwriting. In most cases, these circumstances include losing coverage for other medical needs.

The following are some examples:

- **You Lose Other Health Coverage:** If you go out of coverage under a Medicare Advantage (Part C) plan or if your employer-provided health insurance expires, you may be eligible for guaranteed issue privileges. For instance, if your Medicare Advantage plan departs your service area or if you relocate to an area where the plan is not accessible, you have the option of returning to Original Medicare and purchasing a Medigap plan without having to go through the process of medical underwriting.
- **Your Medigap Plan or Employer Coverage Ends:** If you hold retiree health insurance, a union plan, or COBRA coverage that comes to an end, you are eligible to enroll in a Medigap plan without having to go through the medical underwriting process.
- **Your Insurer Goes Bankrupt or Misleads You:** You may also be eligible for guaranteed issue rights if your Medigap insurance company goes bankrupt or if you lose your policy for reasons that are not your fault (such as receiving incorrect information on your coverage).

How Long You Have to Enroll

The majority of the time, to be eligible for guaranteed issue privileges, you need to apply for Medigap insurance within sixty-three days of losing your former coverage. The insurance company may need medical underwriting after this period has passed.

Switching Medigap Plans

If you are outside of your Open Enrollment Period, it may be more challenging to switch from one Medigap plan to another; however, it is possible to switch policies. In the majority of states, if you transfer plans at a later time, you may be subject to medical underwriting, which may result in increased premiums or the rejection of coverage depending on your health. Certain **states, on the other hand, have regulations that make it simpler for beneficiaries to transfer plans without having to go through the underwriting process.**

- **California and Oregon's Birthday Rule:** The Birthday Rule in California and Oregon allows individuals to transfer to a plan that provides coverage that is equivalent to or less than their current plan during a specific window of time around their birthday each year without being subject to medical underwriting.
- **Missouri's Anniversary Rule:** Beneficiaries in Missouri are permitted to move to a different Medigap plan that offers the same benefits during a 30-day window that coincides with the anniversary of the date on which their initial plan began. This rule is known as the Missouri Anniversary Rule.

Delaying Medigap Enrollment

You may want to postpone enrolling in Medigap in some circumstances, like when you are covered by a union plan or when you have health insurance that is financially supported by your company. Your Medigap Open Enrollment Period will not begin until you enroll in Medicare Part B if you postpone enrolling in Medicare Part B because you are still working and have employer coverage. This is because you are being covered by your employer.

For People Delaying Medicare Part B:
- If you are postponing Medicare Part B because you are still working and have health insurance through your employer, your Medigap Open Enrollment Period will begin when you sign up for Part B after you have left your job or lost coverage through your employer.
- When your job or coverage comes to an end, you will be able to acquire Medigap insurance without having to go through the process of medical underwriting since you will have guaranteed issue rights.

Medigap Enrollment after Retirement

If you retire after the age of 65 and lose your employer-sponsored health insurance, you are eligible to enroll in Medicare Part B and begin your Medigap Open Enrollment Period at that time. Because of your condition, it is essential that you sign up during this period to prevent having your coverage refused or your rates increased. Retirees need to be aware that COBRA coverage, which enables them to retain their employer-provided health insurance for a certain period after leaving a job, is not considered creditable coverage for postponing enrollment in Medicare. When you retire, if you choose to rely on COBRA rather than enrolling in Medicare Part B, you run the risk of incurring penalties and missing out on participation in the Medigap Open Enrollment Period.

When Not to Enroll in Medigap

If you decide to enroll in a Medicare Advantage Plan (Part C), rather than continuing to receive Original Medicare, you will not be required to purchase Medigap coverage. It is not possible to utilize Medigap to cover the out-of-pocket expenses that are associated with Medicare Advantage plans. There is a possibility that you will be able to purchase Medigap coverage if you subsequently decide to transfer back to Original Medicare from Medicare Advantage. However, unless you are eligible for special enrollment rights, you will probably be subject to medical underwriting.

Medigap Plan Pricing and Premiums

The cost of Medigap plans is determined by several criteria, including your age, the state of your health, the location of your home, and the pricing structure that the insurance company uses for its policies. Prescriptions for Medigap insurance are often more expensive than those for

Medicare Advantage plans; nevertheless, they have the advantage of lowering or eliminating unexpected out-of-pocket expenses for treatments that are covered by Medicare.

In general, costs for Medigap policies may be calculated using one of three methods:
- **Community-rated:** Everyone pays the same premium, regardless of age.
- **Issue-age-rated:** Premiums are based on your age at the time you buy the policy. The younger you are when you purchase, the lower your premium will be.
- **Attained-age-rated:** Premiums increase as you get older, making them more expensive over time.

Comparing Costs of Medigap Plans

When picking a Medigap policy, it's essential to know what makes the prices of these plans different. Medigap plans that start with the same letter (e.g., Plan G, Plan N) all give the same basic benefits. However, the prices you pay for these plans can change a lot depending on where you live, your insurance company, and the structure of the plan. You can make a better choice and make sure you get the benefits you need without spending more than you have to if you know about these cost factors.

Standardization of Medigap Plans

To begin, it's important to know that all Medigap plans are the same. In other words, Plan G from one insurance company covers the same things as Plan G from another company, no matter which one costs more. Each Medigap plan covers the same benefits, but the price you pay can be different depending on where you live, your situation, and how the insurance company sets its prices.

Factors That Influence Medigap Costs

1. **Plan Letter and Coverage Levels**

Medigap plans are organized by letter, and each one covers different amounts of costs. It is generally the case that plans with less coverage cost less, while plans with more coverage cost more.
- **Plan A** offers basic coverage and tends to have lower premiums.
- **Plan G** provides more extensive coverage (except for the Part B deductible) and has higher premiums.
- **Plan N** is a cost-effective option, but it includes copayments for doctor visits and emergency room visits.

To compare prices, you need to weigh the cost of the payment against the amount of coverage. Even though plans with lower premiums might look good, they could mean that you have to pay more for healthcare services out of your cash.

2. **Insurance Company Pricing**

Some insurance companies may charge different amounts for the same Medigap plan, even though the plans are all the same. For instance, Plan G from one insurance company might cost a lot more than Plan G from another insurance company, even though they both cover the same things.

- **Shop around and get multiple quotes** from different insurers.
- Use online tools like the **Medicare Plan Finder** to compare costs from different companies.
- Consider factors like customer service, the company's reputation, and financial stability when choosing an insurer, as lower premiums might sometimes come with poorer service.

3. **Geographic Location**

The cost of your Medigap insurance depends a lot on where you live. Rates are different in each state, area, and even ZIP code. Medigap rates are usually higher in places where living costs are higher or where healthcare is more expensive. One example is that Medigap rates may be higher in New York City than in the Midwest. Medigap premiums are controlled in some states to make them cheaper. In others, there may be a bigger range of costs.

4. **Age and Pricing Method Used by the Insurer**

How much a Medigap plan costs may also depend on your age and how the insurance company sets its rates? Different price methods are used by insurers to figure out your premium:

- **Community-Rated (No-Age-Rated):** Everyone, of any age, pays the same premium. This implies that your rate won't go up as you age, but it could go up because of inflation or something else.
- **Issue-Age-Rated (Entry-Age-Rated):** This is called issue-age-rated or entry-age-rated. Your fee will be less if you sign up when you are younger. Rates don't go up as you get older, but they might go up because of inflation.
- **Attained-Age-Rated:** Your payment is based on your age right now, and it goes up as you age. Younger recipients may have cheap premiums at first, but they can go up a lot over time. Plans with an attained age rating have the lowest rates at first, but they may cost more in the long run.

Ask the insurance company how they set their prices if you want to compare prices. Attained-age plans may look less expensive at first, but as you get older, they may cost more. Community-rated or issue-age-rated insurance, on the other hand, has rates that are easier to plan for over time.

5. **Inflation and Annual Rate Increases**

Most of the time, Medigap rates stay the same from year to year. However, they can go up if prices for healthcare or inflation rise. Insurance companies may raise your rates every year, even if your insurance doesn't have an age limit. Rate hikes can be very different from one insurance company to the next, so it's important to find out how often a company has raised rates before you choose a plan. Some insurance companies may have a past of raising rates often or by a large amount, while others may have more stable prices. If you look into how often the insurance company raises rates in the past, you can pick a plan with more stable long-term costs.

Comparing Medigap Costs: Steps to Follow

To make sure you're getting the best coverage at the best price when you compare Medigap costs, do these things:

1. **Identify Your Coverage Needs**

Figure out which Medigap plan letter gives you the coverage you need. For instance, Plan G or Plan F (if you're qualified) might be your best bet if you want full coverage with low out-of-pocket costs. With Plan N, you might be able to save money on your rates if you are ready to make some copayments.

2. **Compare Premiums Across Multiple Insurers**

Once you've picked a plan letter (like Plan G), get quotes on premiums from several insurers in your area. Compare the prices of different Medicare plans with the help of online tools or a Medicare dealer.

3. **Consider Pricing Methods**

Pay close attention to how each insurance company sets its prices. Attained-age plans might look cheaper at first, but they might cost more as you get older. Community-rated or issue-age-rated plans may have higher rates at first, but they offer more stable costs over time.

4. **Research the Insurer's Reputation**

Find out how financially stable each insurer is and how well they treat their customers. While a cheap insurance company may offer good service, they may not be the best choice in the long run.

5. **Understand Additional Costs**

Think about other possible costs, like copayments, coinsurance, and deductibles. Some Medigap plans cover almost all of your out-of-pocket costs, but others may charge you extra for things like doctor visits or trips to the emergency room. Make sure you know how much your health care will cost in total, not just the monthly fee.

6. **Consider Future Rate Increases**

Ask the insurance company about their past rate hikes. Even if the first payment is low, companies whose rates have gone up a lot in the past might not be the best choice. A lot of the time, keeping prices stable is more important than getting the cheapest rate up front.

7. **Check for Discounts**

Some insurance companies offer lower Medigap rates. For instance, if you and your partner both buy Medigap insurance from the same company, you might both get a discount. You might get more savings if you pay your fee once a year instead of every month or if you use electronic funds transfers (EFT) to pay.

Considering Your Budget and Health Needs

It's important to compare Medigap plans by comparing the fees to the level of coverage and the amount of medical care you expect to need.

To get the best price and service, do the following:
- **If You're Healthy:** If you're healthy and don't think you'll need a lot of medical care, you might want a cheaper plan like Plan N or a high-deductible form of Plan F or Plan G, if they're available. The rates for these plans are lower, but you may have to pay more out of pocket if you need care.
- **If You Have Chronic Health Conditions:** If you have a long-term illness, a more complete plan like Plan G might be better for you if you think you will need a lot of medical care or hospital stays. You may have to pay more for payments, but you'll have less to pay out of pocket for healthcare.
- **If You're Concerned About Future Costs:** If you're worried that your rates will go up as you get older, you might want to look into community-rated or issue-age-rated insurance. The rates for these plans are more stable over time, which can help with planning your long-term spending.

Special Considerations for High-Deductible Medigap Plans

Some insurance companies offer high-deductible forms of Medigap plans, like Plan F and Plan G, in addition to the regular plans. They have a high cost ($2,740 in 2024) that you have to meet before the plan starts to pay for treatments. You'll pay a lot less each month for these plans, but you'll have to pay for most services yourself until your deductible is met. **A high-deductible Medigap plan can be a good option if:**
- You're generally healthy and don't expect to use a lot of medical services.
- You're comfortable taking on more out-of-pocket risk in exchange for lower premiums.

If you do need major medical care, you will need to pay the deductible before the plan starts to cover your costs.

CHAPTER 7
PREVENTIVE SERVICES COVERED BY MEDICARE

Screenings, Vaccinations, and Annual Wellness Visits

Medicare gives its recipients a lot of services that help them stay healthy and find health problems early on. Some of these services are screenings, vaccines, and an annual wellness visit. They are all meant to keep people healthy and stop them from getting major illnesses. Some people who use these services have better health results and may end up spending less on healthcare in the long run.

Medicare-Covered Screenings

Screenings are checks or tests that find health problems before they show signs. Medicare Part B covers several screening programs that look for early signs of illnesses and conditions like osteoporosis, cancer, heart disease, and diabetes. These are some of the most important screenings that Medicare pays for:

Cancer Screenings

- **Mammograms:** Women ages 40 and up can get a screening mammogram once a year through Medicare. Diagnostic scans, which are used to check up on results that aren't normal, are also covered, but you may have to pay a copayment.
- **Cervical and Vaginal Cancer Screening:** Women with Medicare can get a Pap test and pelvic screening, which includes a clinical breast check, once every 24 months, or once every 12 months if they are at high risk for cancer.
- **Colorectal Cancer Screenings:** Medicare covers several screening tests based on your risk level to find colorectal cancer early:
    - **Fecal Occult Blood Test** once every 12 months.
    - **Colonoscopy** every 10 years (or every 2 years if you're at high risk).
    - **Flexible Sigmoidoscopy** every 4 years (or every 10 years if you've had a colonoscopy).
- **Prostate Cancer Screening:** Men aged 50 and up can get a Prostate-Specific Antigen (PSA) test and a digital rectal exam every year through Medicare.

Cardiovascular Screenings

- **Cardiovascular Disease Screenings:** Every 5 years, Medicare pays for blood tests to look for diseases like high cholesterol, lipid disorders, and triglyceride levels that could lead to heart disease.

- **Abdominal Aortic Aneurysm Screening:** People who are at risk for an abdominal aortic aneurysm can get an ultrasound for free through Medicare. Men aged 65 to 75 who have smoked at least 100 cigarettes in their lives are at risk, as well as people in their family who have always smoked.

Diabetes Screening

- **Diabetes Screening Tests:** People who are at risk for diabetes can get up to two diabetes screenings a year paid for by Medicare. High blood pressure, high cholesterol, being overweight, or having a history of high blood sugar is all things that put you at risk.
- **Diabetes Self-Management Training:** If you have been identified with diabetes, Medicare also pays for training to help you learn how to take care of your condition and avoid problems.

Bone Density Testing

- **Osteoporosis Screening:** Medicare covers a bone density test (bone mass measurement) every 24 months for people who are at risk of osteoporosis or who have certain conditions, like not getting enough estrogen or having a history of breaking bones.

Other Screenings

- **HIV Screening:** Medicare covers HIV screening once a year for people who are more likely to get HIV, including pregnant women, or up to three times during pregnancy.
- **Depression Screening:** Medicare covers a depression screening once a year at a general care office to help find depression early.
- **Obesity Screening and Counseling:** Medicare pays for screening and counseling for obesity for people with a body mass index (BMI) of 30 or more, to help them lose weight and improve their health in general.

Vaccinations Covered by Medicare

Getting vaccinated, also called vaccinations, is the only way to avoid getting dangerous diseases. Several important vaccines are covered by Medicare Parts B and D; these help protect you from getting diseases that can make you very sick or require treatment.

Flu Shot

- **Annual Influenza Vaccine (Flu Shot):** Medicare covers the flu shot once a flu season, which is usually in the fall or winter. Older people need to get the flu shot even more because they are more likely to get symptoms from the flu, like asthma.

Pneumonia Vaccine

- **Pneumococcal Vaccination:** The PCV13 (Prevnar 13) and PPSV23 (Pneumovax 23) vaccines are two types of pneumonia vaccines that Medicare pays. Most adults will only need these shots once, but people who are very likely to get pneumonia may need both.

Hepatitis B Vaccine

- **Hepatitis B Vaccine:** Medicare covers the Hepatitis B vaccine for people who are at a medium to high risk for getting Hepatitis B, like those with diabetes, end-stage kidney disease, or hemophilia. Three shots are used to give the vaccinations.

Shingles Vaccine (Not Covered by Part B)

- **Shingles (Herpes Zoster) Vaccine:** While the flu or pneumonia vaccines are covered by Medicare Part B, the shingles vaccine is not; however, it is usually covered by Medicare Part D. This vaccine helps protect against shingles and its complications, especially postherpetic neuralgia, a painful condition that can happen after shingles.

COVID-19 Vaccine

- **COVID-19 Vaccine:** All Medicare beneficiaries are covered for COVID-19 vaccinations, including repeat shots, through Medicare Part B. This is true no matter where they get the vaccine (e.g., drugstore, clinic, or doctor's office).

Medicare-Covered Annual Wellness Visit

Medicare Part B covers more than just screenings and vaccinations. It also covers an Annual Wellness Visit that is meant to help you make a specific plan for staying healthy. You can only get the Welcome to Medicare screening visit in the first year after signing up for Medicare Part B. This visit is not the same as that one.

What Happens During an Annual Wellness Visit?

Your healthcare provider will do the following during the Annual Wellness Visit:
- **Review Your Medical and Family History:** This will help you figure out if there have been any changes or new risk factors in the last year.
- **Update a List of Current Medications and Providers:** Your doctor will go over all of your medications, including prescription drugs, over-the-counter drugs, and vitamins. They will also make a new list of the healthcare providers you see regularly.
- **Create a Personalized Prevention Plan:** Your doctor will make a prevention plan for you based on your health and risk factors. This plan could include suggestions for more tests, shots, changes to your lifestyle, or references to experts.
- **Measure Your Vital Signs:** This means taking your height, weight, blood pressure, and maybe some other basic health signs.
- **Conduct Cognitive Assessments:** Your doctor may do a simple test to see how well your brain is working and look for signs of dementia or memory loss.

Why the Annual Wellness Visit is Important

The Annual Wellness Visit is a very important time to talk to your provider about your health and focus on preventive care. It helps you figure out ways to improve your health, like taking care of chronic diseases, losing weight, or giving up smoking. It also makes sure you get all the necessary tests and vaccines.

Costs for Preventive Services Under Medicare

Medicare Part B pays for all your preventive care as long as you go to a therapist who accepts Medicare assignment. This means that you don't have to pay a deductible or copayment. **There are, however, a few important things to remember about costs:**
- **Additional Testing or Follow-Up Care:** If a screening leads to a diagnosis (for example, if a colonoscopy finds polyps that need to be removed), Medicare may consider the test diagnostic, and you may have to pay a copayment or coinsurance for the follow-up care.
- **Vaccines Covered Under Part D:** Some vaccines, like the shingles vaccine, are paid by Part D and not Part B. Depending on your Part D plan, you may have to pay a copayment or share when you get these vaccines.
- **Annual Wellness Visit Costs:** The Annual Wellness Visit is free, but you may be charged for extra services if you talk about any new or current health problems during the visit.

Preventive Services without Copay or Deductible

A lot of different preventive services are covered by Medicare Part B. These services help people stay healthy and find possible health problems early on. A lot of these services are free for Medicare beneficiaries, which means they don't have to pay a copay or payment as long as they get them from a healthcare provider that accepts Medicare assignments. The goal of these services is to keep people from getting sick or to find them early when they can be treated most effectively. **Here is a full list of all the free preventive services that Medicare covers, such as health visits, tests, and vaccines.**

1. **Annual Wellness Visit**

What It Covers: The Annual Wellness Visit is a checkup that focuses on preventive care once a year. Your health, medical background, medicines, and vital signs will be looked at, and a specific prevention plan will be made to help you take care of your health.

Frequency: Once every 12 months.

Cost: If the visit is only for preventive care, there is no copay or deductible. There may be extra costs, though, if other health problems are dealt with during the stay.

2. **Welcome to Medicare Preventive Visit**

What It Covers: This is a one-time preventive visit that you can get within the first 12 months of signing up for Medicare Part B. It includes a review of your medical and family history, a list of preventive services, and personalized health advice.

Frequency: Once in the first year of signing up for Medicare Part B.

Cost: No copay or deductible.

3. **Cancer Screenings**

Mammogram (Breast Cancer Screening)

- **What It Covers:** A screening mammogram for women to detect breast cancer.
- **Frequency:** Once every 12 months for women aged 40 and older; once every 12 months for women under 40 who are at high risk?
- **Cost:** No copay or deductible for screening mammograms.

Cervical and Vaginal Cancer Screening (Pap test and Pelvic Exam)

- **What It Covers:** It includes Pap tests, pelvic checks, and clinical breast exams for women to find cancer in the cervix and vagina.
- **Frequency:** For most women, it's done once every 24 months. For women at high risk or of childbearing age with abnormal Pap test results, it's done once every 12 months.
- **Cost:** No copay or deductible.

Colorectal Cancer Screenings

- **What It Covers:** Different tests to find colorectal cancer, like colonoscopy, fecal hidden blood tests, and flexible sigmoidoscopy.
- **Frequency:**
  - **Fecal Occult Blood Test:** Once every 12 months.
  - **Flexible Sigmoidoscopy:** Once every 4 years.
  - **Colonoscopy:** Once every 10 years (or every 2 years if at high risk).

- **Cost:** There is no copay or deductible for these screenings, but there may be extra costs if polyps are found and removed during a colonoscopy.

Prostate Cancer Screening

- **What It Covers:** Prostate-Specific Antigen (PSA) test for men to detect prostate cancer.
- **Frequency:** Once every 12 months for men aged 50 and older.
- **Cost:** No copay or deductible for the PSA test.

4. **Cardiovascular Screenings**

What It Covers: Triglycerides, cholesterol, and fat levels can be checked in the blood to help find conditions that may cause heart disease.

Frequency: Once every 5 years.

Cost: No copay or deductible.

5. **Diabetes Screenings**

What It Covers: Blood tests can check for diabetes if you are at risk, like if you have high blood pressure, high cholesterol, are overweight, or have had high blood sugar in the past.

Frequency: Up to two screenings a year for people who are at high risk for diabetes.

Cost: No copay or deductible.

6. **Bone Density Screening (Osteoporosis Screening)**

What It Covers: Bone mass readings to find osteoporosis and figure out how strong bones are.

Frequency: Once every 24 months for people who are at risk, like women who don't get enough estrogen or people who have had broken bones in the past.

Cost: No copay or deductible.

7. **Vaccinations**

Influenza (Flu) Vaccine

- **What It Covers:** An annual flu shot to protect against influenza.
- **Frequency:** Once per flu season.
- **Cost:** No copay or deductible.

Pneumococcal Vaccine

- **What It Covers:** Vaccines that protect against pneumonia, such as the PCV13 (Prevnar 13) and PPSV23 (Pneumovax 23) vaccines.
- **Frequency:** Most people only need these shots once in their whole lives.
- **Cost:** No copay or deductible.

Hepatitis B Vaccine

- **What It Covers:** A set of shots to protect people at medium or high risk from getting Hepatitis B.
- **Frequency:** Covered if you meet certain risk factors.
- **Cost:** No copay or deductible for eligible individuals.

COVID-19 Vaccine

- **What It Covers:** COVID-19 shots and boosts.
- **Frequency:** Based on what the Centers for Disease Control and Prevention (CDC) says.
- **Cost:** No copay or deductible.

8. **HIV Screening**

What It Covers: People who are more likely to get HIV, like pregnant women, are screened for it.

Frequency: Once a year, or up to three times while pregnant.

Cost: No copay or deductible.

9. **Depression Screening**

What It Covers: A screening for depression in a primary care setting.

Frequency: Once every 12 months.

Cost: No copay or deductible.

10. **Tobacco Use Cessation Counseling**

What It Covers: Counseling sessions to help individuals quit smoking or using tobacco.

Frequency: Eight counseling sessions in 12 months for those who use tobacco.

Cost: No copay or deductible.

11. **Obesity Screening and Counseling**

What It Covers: People with a body mass index (BMI) of 30 or higher can get screenings and guidance to help them control their weight and lower their risk of diseases linked to obesity.

Frequency: Based on need.

Cost: No copay or deductible.

12. **Alcohol Misuse Screening and Counseling**

What It Covers: It includes tests to see if someone is abusing alcohol and counseling meetings for people who drink too much but aren't hooked on it.

Frequency: once a year for screening and up to four in-person therapy sessions a year.

Cost: No copay or deductible.

13. **Abdominal Aortic Aneurysm Screening**

What It Covers: An ultrasound that is done just once to look for abdominal aortic aneurysms, which are lumps in the artery that can burst.

Frequency: Once, for guys aged 65 to 75 who have smoked at least 100 cigarettes in their lives or for people who have a history of aneurysms in their family?

Cost: No copay or deductible for eligible individuals.

14. **Glaucoma Test**

What It Covers: A glaucoma test for people who are at high risk, like those with a family history of glaucoma, African Americans aged 50 or older, or Hispanics aged 65 or older.

Frequency: Once every twelve months.

Cost: You may have to pay a 20% copayment and the Part B fee unless you meet other requirements that let you get a test for free.

15. **Counseling for Sexually Transmitted Infections (STIs)**

What It Covers: Advice on sexually transmitted diseases (STIs) and tests for chlamydia, gonorrhea, syphilis, and hepatitis B for people who are at risk.

Frequency: Annually for those at risk.
Cost: No copay or deductible.

Importance of Regular Health Check-ups

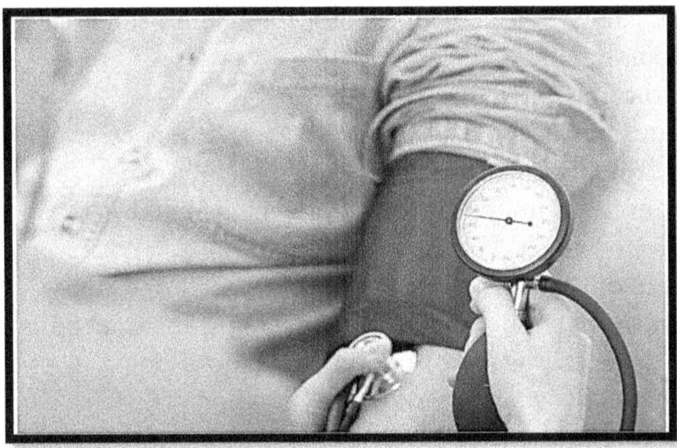

It's easy to get caught up in the busyness of daily life and forget about our health, which is the most important thing. A lot of people don't pay much attention to their health until they have a problem. In situations like these, getting regular check-ups is important because they help you stay healthy and avoid problems before they happen. This blog post will talk about why it's so important for people to make regular check-ups a priority. This can be a habit that saves lives.

1. **Early Detection of Health Issues**

Getting regular check-ups is like getting a report card on your health. They can help find health problems early on when they are easiest to deal with. A lot of diseases, like cancer and diabetes, don't have any signs at first. When signs do show up, the disease may have already gotten a lot worse. By getting regular check-ups, problems can be found early, which increases the chances of good treatment and healing.

2. **Prevention is Better than Cure**

It is true in the world of health care that prevention is better than cure. At regular check-ups, doctors can look at your risk factors and give you advice on how to make changes to your lifestyle that can help keep you from getting sick. Early action can make a big difference in your health, whether it's changing your food, getting more exercise, or giving up smoking.

3. **Monitoring Chronic Conditions**

People who already have long-term illnesses like diabetes, high blood pressure, or heart disease need to get annual check-ups. They let doctors see how the situation is getting worse, change treatment plans, and keep problems from happening. Chronic diseases can make a person's quality of life a lot better if they are managed properly.

4. **Immunizations and Vaccinations**

Getting vaccinated is an important part of protective health care. Regular check-ups make sure you have all of your necessary shots, which protects you from diseases that can be prevented with vaccines. This is especially important for kids, the old, and people whose immunity systems aren't working well.

5. Establishing a Baseline for Health

Check-ups regularly help you figure out how healthy you are in general. A doctor or nurse can keep track of how your vital signs, blood pressure, cholesterol levels, and other health markers change over time. This knowledge is very helpful for finding small changes that could mean there are health problems deeper down.

6. Reducing Healthcare Costs

Getting regular check-ups may seem like an extra cost, but they can help keep healthcare costs down in the long run. Finding and stopping problems early can save you a lot of money on treatments, hospital stays, and medicines that you might need if the problem isn't found in time.

7. Promoting Peace of Mind

It can be relaxing to know that you are constantly taking steps to keep an eye on and improve your health. Checkups give you peace of mind that you are doing everything you can to stay healthy and let you know right away if there are any problems.

8. Setting a Good Example

Finally, your dedication to regular check-ups can show your family and friends how to live a healthy life. Telling your friends and family to put their health first can have a positive effect on the whole community, creating a culture of wellness.

CHAPTER 8

NAVIGATING MEDICARE CLAIMS AND APPEALS

How to File a Medicare Claim

Most of the time, your healthcare providers and sellers will file your Medicare claims for you. However, there are times when you may need to do it yourself. For instance, if you go to a doctor who doesn't file your claims or get services outside of the U.S., you might need to do something to make sure Medicare pays for the services it covers.

When to File a Medicare Claim

Health care providers and suppliers who accept Medicare assignments have to send claims straight to Medicare, so you don't have to worry about filing a claim most of the time. **That being said, there are times when you might need to file your claim:**

- **Provider or Supplier Doesn't File the Claim:** If your healthcare provider or supplier doesn't file the claim for you, you will have to do it yourself with Medicare. This doesn't happen very often, but it can happen with some sellers or providers who don't take Medicare.
- **Services outside the U.S.:** You may need to claim if you get medical care while going outside of the U.S. because Medicare may cover those services (in some cases).
- **Services Provided by Foreign Hospitals:** Medicare may pay for inpatient hospital care if you live in the U.S. but are closer to a foreign hospital, or if you need to go to a foreign hospital right away because it's closer than the closest U.S. hospital in an emergency.
- **Delayed Claim Filing by Provider:** If your provider or seller doesn't file the claim within 12 months of when you got the service, you can do it yourself.

What Information You'll Need to File a Medicare Claim

To file a Medicare claim, you'll need certain papers and details to make sure the claim is handled correctly. Here are the most important papers and information you'll need:

- **Medicare Summary Notice (MSN):** This is a list of the health care services and things that Medicare has paid for. It's sent to you every three months. This lets you check to see if your service or seller has sent in your claim.
- **CMS Form 1490S (Patient's Request for Medical Payment):** This is what you will use to make your own Medicare claim. You can find it on the Medicare website and print or download it.
- **Itemized Bill or Statement:** You need to include a bill from your healthcare source or seller that lists all of the following:
  - The date of service.
  - A description of the medical services or supplies received.
  - The provider's name, address, and National Provider Identifier (NPI) number.
  - The provider's signature.
  - The cost of each service or item.
- **Medicare Beneficiary Information:** You will need to give your Medicare Number, which can be found on your Medicare card.
- **Other Health Insurance Information (if applicable):** If you have other insurance, like Medicaid, an employer-provided plan, or Medigap, you should list it on the claim form. Medicare may be able to group funds with other types of insurance.

How to File a Medicare Claim

To file a Medicare claim on your own, do these things:

Step 1: Get the Itemized Bill from Your Provider

Ask your healthcare provider or seller for a bill or statement with a list of all the services or goods they gave you. Make sure that the bill has all the necessary details, like the date of service, a description of the service, and the National Provider Identification (NPI) number.

Step 2: Download and Complete CMS Form 1490S

You need to fill out CMS Form 1490S, which is called a **Patient's Request for Medical Payment**. On the Medicare.gov page, you can download this form.

This is how you fill out CMS Form 1490S:

- **Section 1:** Give your name, address, and Medicare number (found on your Medicare card) as well as other personal details.
- **Section 2:** Describe the good or service you got. Be clear about what kind of medical service or thing you got and why you got it.
- **Section 3:** In Section 3, list any other health insurance you have, like Medigap, Medicaid, or health insurance through your job.
- **Section 4:** Attach to the form the itemized bill or statement from your healthcare source or seller. Make sure the bill has all the important details, like the name, address, and NPI number of the service.

- **Section 5:** Sign and date the form.

Step 3: Include Supporting Documentation

Along with the finished claim form and itemized bill, you should also send any other paperwork that Medicare might need to handle the claim. Such things could be:

- Explanation of Benefits (EOB) from your other insurance, if applicable.
- Copies of medical records, if requested.

Step 4: Submit the Claim

Send CMS Form 1490S, filled out, along with the detailed bill and any supporting files, to the Medicare agent in your state who handles claims. You can call 1-800-MEDICARE (1-800-633-4227) or look at the Medicare.gov page to find the right address for your claims.

Filing Deadlines

It's important to file Medicare claims promptly. The last day to file a Medicare claim is 12 months after the service. For instance, if you got medical care on October 1, 2023, you have until October 1, 2024 to submit the claim. You might have to pay for the services yourself if you miss the date. Medicare might not pay for them.

What Happens After You File a Claim

A Medicare Administrative Contractor (MAC) will review your claim once you send it in. The agent will look over the claim and see if Medicare will pay for the goods or services. You'll get a Medicare Summary Notice (MSN) after the claim is handled. **This will tell you how much Medicare paid and how much you may owe.**

- If Medicare agrees with the claim, it will pay your healthcare provider or you directly for its part of the costs.
- If Medicare says no to the claim, you can appeal the decision. There will be information on how to make an appeal in the denial notice along with the reason for the denial.

Medicare Appeals Process

There is a way to appeal if Medicare denies your claim or if you don't agree with the amount paid. **There are several steps in the complaints process, but the first one is to ask that the claim be looked at again. To do this:**

- **Submit an appeal request** in writing within **120 days** of receiving your Medicare Summary Notice (MSN).
- **Include a detailed explanation** of why you believe Medicare should have paid for the service or why you disagree with the amount paid.

The appeals process can take a while, but it's important to go through it if you think Medicare should pay for the service.

Key Tips for Filing a Medicare Claim

- **Check with Your Provider First:** Before you file a claim on your own, make sure your healthcare provider or seller plans to send the claim to Medicare by calling them. This can help you save time and work if the service already does it.
- **Keep Copies of All Documents:** Always make copies of your claim form, your detailed bills, and any other paperwork that backs up your claim. This could be useful if you need to get back in touch with Medicare or fight a decision.
- **Track the Claim:** Once you've sent in your claim, you can check on its progress through your MyMedicare.gov account or by calling 1-800-MEDICARE.

What to do if a Service is denied

It can be annoying and stressful when Medicare doesn't pay for a medical service, treatment, or item. You can appeal the ruling, though, if you think the service should have been paid. The Medicare appeals process lets people whose claims were rejected ask for a review of the decision. If Medicare says no to a service, this is a complete help on what to do, how to appeal, the steps needed, and what to expect.

1. **Understand the Reason for Denial**

First, you need to know why Medicare turned down the service. If you have Original Medicare, you'll get a Medicare Summary Notice (MSN). If you have a Medicare Advantage (Part C) or Part D (prescription drug) plan, you'll get an Explanation of Benefits (EOB). These letters tell you what services you got, how much Medicare paid, and how much you may still owe.

- **Review the Medicare Summary Notice (MSN):** The MSN tells you in detail what services were refused and why. Some common reasons are:
    - The service is not considered medically necessary.
    - The service is not covered under Medicare.
    - The provider did not submit enough information to justify coverage.
    - The service was performed by a provider not approved by Medicare.
- **Check for Errors:** Denials can happen because of mistakes made by staff, like wrong code or missing information. Before you file an appeal, talk to your healthcare expert to make sure the information is correct. They might be able to fix the problem by sending in updated information.

2. **Determine the Type of Medicare Coverage You Have**

How you appeal depends on what kind of Medicare benefits you have. If you have **Original Medicare,** a **Medicare Advantage Plan (Part C),** or a **Medicare Prescription Drug Plan (Part D),** the process is a little different.

Original Medicare (Part A and Part B): If Original Medicare denies a service; the appeal process starts with Medicare.

Medicare Advantage (Part C): If your Medicare Advantage plan denies coverage, you need to appeal directly with your plan. Medicare Advantage plans have to follow Medicare's rules for appeals, but they also have their ways of handling them.

Medicare Part D (Prescription Drug Coverage): If your Medicare Part D plan denies a prescription drug, you can appeal to your Part D provider.

3. **Gather Supporting Documentation**

Get any proof that supports your claim together before you file your appeal. These things could be:

Medical Records: Ask your doctor or nurse to give you any medical records or notes that show the denied service was medically necessary.

Doctor's Letter: A letter from your doctor describing why the service, treatment, or item is medically important can help your appeal a lot.

Previous Authorizations or Approvals: If Medicare or your plan approved the same service before; you should include proof of that approval.

4. **File a Medicare Appeal: The Steps**

The steps you need to take to appeal a Medicare claim denial depend on whether you have Original Medicare, a Medicare Advantage Plan, or a Medicare Prescription Drug Plan.

A. Appealing a Denial under the Original Medicare

If your Original Medicare claim was denied, do these things:

Step 1: Request a Redetermination

If your claim was denied, you can ask the Medicare Administrative Contractor (MAC) to review it. This is called a **redetermination**. You have 120 days from the date you get your Medicare Summary Notice (MSN) to request the redetermination.

To file the appeal:

- Complete the **Redetermination Request Form (CMS-20027)**, or simply write a letter that includes:
    - Your name, Medicare number, and contact information.
    - A description of the denied service and the reason you disagree with the denial.
    - A copy of the MSN showing the denial, with the specific denied claim highlighted.
    - Any supporting documents, such as medical records or a letter from your doctor.
- Send the appeal request and supporting documents to the address listed on your MSN.

Step 2: Receive the Decision

If you ask for a redetermination, the Medicare contractor has 60 days to reply. They will either approve the claim and issue payment or uphold the denial and provide an explanation. You can go to the next level of appeal if your first one was denied.

B. Appealing a Denial under Medicare Advantage (Part C)

If your Medicare Advantage Plan says it won't pay for a treatment or service, do these things:

Step 1: File an Appeal with Your Plan

You have 60 days from the time you get the Explanation of Benefits (EOB) or denial notice to file an appeal with your Medicare Advantage Plan. You can write a letter or use the plan's unique appeal form. **In the letter, you should include the following:**

- Your name, Medicare number, and contact information.
- A detailed description of the denied service and why you believe it should be covered.
- A copy of the denial notice or EOB, with the denied service highlighted.
- Supporting documents, such as medical records or a doctor's letter.

Send the request for an appeal to the address your plan gives you. For normal reviews, Medicare Advantage plans have to decide within 30 days. If you need an answer quickly, they have to do so within 72 hours.

Step 2: Independent Review

If your plan denies your appeal, you can ask for a review by a Medicare-approved independent group. The independent reviewer will make a choice based on the steps you outline in your plan for asking for this review.

C. Appealing a Denial under Medicare Part D (Prescription Drug Plan)

If your Medicare Part D plan denies a prescription drug or limits what it will cover, do these things:

Step 1: Request a Coverage Determination

Start by requesting a **coverage determination** from your Part D plan. That is, you have to ask your insurance company to cover the medicine or lift a coverage limit (like step therapy or prior permission).

- Call your plan or submit a **Coverage Determination Request Form**.
- Include supporting documentation, such as a letter from your doctor explaining why you need the medication.

Your plan must respond within **72 hours** (24 hours for expedited requests).

Step 2: Appeal the Coverage Decision

You can ask your Part D plan for an appeal, which is also known as a **redetermination** if your coverage determination is denied. You have 60 days from the date you got the denial to file this appeal. The plan will look over your case and decide within 7 days (or 72 hours if you need it faster). If the plan denies your appeal, you can request an independent review.

5. **The Five Levels of Medicare Appeals**

There are five levels to the Medicare appeal process. You can go to the next level for more review if your claim is denied at any level:

- **Redetermination by the Medicare Administrative Contractor (MAC):** A first-level review of your claim by the contractor that processes Medicare claims.
- **Reconsideration by a Qualified Independent Contractor (QIC):** A second-level review by a different contractor than the one that denied the claim.
- **Administrative Law Judge (ALJ) Hearing:** You can ask for a hearing before an Administrative Law Judge if the amount in question is at least $200 in 2024.
- **Medicare Appeals Council Review:** You can ask the Medicare Appeals Council to look over the Administrative Law Judge's decision again if you don't agree with it.
- **Judicial Review in Federal Court:** You can go to federal court with your appeal if the amount in question is at least $2,000 in 2024.

6. **Keep Track of Deadlines**

At each step of the Medicare appeals process, there are several due dates. If you don't send in your appeals on time, you could lose your right to appeal.

7. **Get Help with Your Appeal**

You don't have to go through the appeals process by yourself. You can get help from the following:

- **State Health Insurance Assistance Program (SHIP):** SHIP can help you with Medicare problems, such as appeals, for free and without bias.
- **1-800-MEDICARE:** Call Medicare to find out more about your rights and get help appealing.
- **Medicare.gov:** The official Medicare website has a lot of information on how to appeal, such as forms and directions that you can download.

Medicare Appeals Process Explained

Individuals who are registered with Medicare are afforded certain rights and safeguards about the medical treatments they receive. Among these rights is the ability to challenge decisions made by Medicare. It gives a person the opportunity to appeal a decision made by Medicare over the denial of coverage or late payments, which may result in fines. A distinct review procedure is carried out for each of the five levels that make up the Medicare appeals process. As soon as Medicare grants approval for an appeal at the initial level, the procedure is terminated. As an alternative, the procedure may go to the subsequent level, and so on, if Medicare rejects the original appeal. To prove their appeal case to Medicare, an individual is required to obtain supporting documentation from their physician or another kind of medical expert. Medicare will receive these papers, in addition to the appeal form, from the individual involved.

What are the reasons for appealing?

If individuals express disagreement with Medicare's decision to not approve the following, they have the opportunity to file an appeal.

- An application for a medical service, supply, item, or prescription medication that Medicare ought to pay for
- An application for payment for a healthcare service, supply, item, or prescription medicine that they have already obtained
- A request to alter the amount that a person is required to pay for a healthcare service, supply, item, or prescription pill

The following are some of the reasons why Medicare could deny coverage:

- There is no medical necessity for the product, service, or prescription medication in question.
- One of the individuals does not fulfill the conditions necessary to be eligible for coverage.
- At no point in time does Medicare fund the item, service, or prescription that is being discussed.

Appealing monthly premium penalties

An individual also can appeal Medicare's penalty decisions.

Late enrollment penalty

A late enrollment penalty is imposed by Medicare if an individual does not enroll in Original Medicare (parts A and B) or Part D when they initially become eligible for the program, or if the individual does not have any alternative coverage from another source. In the event that a person received health insurance via their workplace yet Medicare fined them a late enrollment penalty, the individual can appeal the decision on their behalf. One of the pieces of evidence that will be required to appeal is evidence that demonstrates appropriate coverage equivalent to that of Medicare.

Income-related monthly adjustment amount surcharge

To determine the Medicare Part B and Part D premiums, Medicare takes into consideration the individual's income as it was reported on their tax return from two years ago. There is an additional fee that is applied to the basic premiums which is known as the Medicare income-related monthly adjustment amount (IRMAA). If an individual differs from Medicare's evaluation, they can file an appeal about an IRMAA surcharge.

Types of notice

A Medicare beneficiary is considered to have initiated the appeal process when they are provided with an official written notification that Medicare has denied coverage.

Standard notice types include:
- **Medicare summary notice:** This provides information regarding Medicare payments for covered services and products for the preceding three months. In addition, it expresses if Medicare does not cover any certain item or service.
- **Advance Beneficiary Notice of Noncoverage (ABN):** An advanced beneficiary notice of noncoverage, also known as an ABN, is a notification that is sent by doctors and other healthcare professionals and suppliers to provide an advanced warning that Medicare might not cover a certain treatment or medication.
- **Skilled Nursing Facility Advance Beneficiary Notice (SNF ABN):** The facility will give the SNF ABN to the individual who is currently residing in a skilled nursing facility and is getting close to the maximum number of days that are covered by the facility's insurance policy.
- **Fee-for-Service Advance Beneficiary Notice (FFS ABN):** A Fee-for-Service Advance Beneficiary Notice (FFS ABN) is a notice that informs an individual that Medicare will charge them for a service that they have received or are scheduled to receive in the future.
- **Notice of Denial of Medical Coverage (Integrated Denial Notice):** These notices are sent by Medicare Advantage plans and Medicaid if they will not cover any portion of a treatment.
- **Hospital Issued Notice of Noncoverage (HINN):** This form is utilized by hospitals if Medicare coverage for inpatient stays is in the process of expiring.
- **Notice of Medicare Non-Coverage (NOMNC):** This notice is comparable to the HINN, but it discusses inpatient treatment that is provided in a skilled nursing facility (SNF), rehabilitation facility, or hospice in place of hospice care. At the very least, 2 days before the coverage expires, this will be delivered to the individual.

Starting the appeal process

Information on the appeals procedure is included in the notices that Medicare sends out to its beneficiaries. **On the other hand, the various Medicare components each have their unique procedures for initiating an appeal, which are as follows:**

- **Original Medicare (Parts A and B)**: If you disagree with a coverage or payment decision under **Original Medicare**, the first step is to fill out a **Redetermination Request form**. This form is used to ask Medicare to reconsider its initial decision. The request should be submitted to the Medicare Administrative Contractor (MAC) that handled your claim.
- **Medicare Part D (Prescription Drug Coverage)**: For **Medicare Part D** appeals, individuals must also start by submitting a **Redetermination Request form** to request a review of the decision. This is typically used when a prescription drug isn't covered or the cost is higher than expected.
- **Medicare Advantage (Part C)**: **Medicare Advantage** plans follow a different process for appeals, as they are offered by private insurers. To appeal a decision related to a Medicare Advantage plan, you'll need to contact your **plan provider** directly. Each provider may have its own specific procedures, so it's important to get detailed instructions from your plan about how to submit an appeal.

Every form for appealing a decision includes some basic personal information as well as specifics about the allegation. Individuals are required to provide specifics on the service or item that they are appealing to, as well as the reasons why they believe Medicare's decision is inappropriate. They also need to present evidence in support of their claim, such as a letter from a physician, test results, or information regarding the diagnosis.

Decision notification limits

Notifications of decisions are subject to a variety of time limits. Generally speaking, Medicare will issue a decision within sixty days after receiving the appeal submitted to them. A pre-service request can take up to 14 days to be processed, while an expedited service request might take anywhere from 24 to 72 hours.

Medicare appeal levels

There are five different levels in the Medicare appeals procedure. If an individual is not satisfied with a judgment made at any level, the appeal will be transferred to the subsequent level of review. Medicare gives out a decision letter at each level, which provides information about the further measures that need to be taken. **This is how the levels are composed:**

- **Level 1:** This level is called redetermination. It is an initial review by a Medicare administrative contractor.
- **Level 2:** A qualified independent contractor reviews the appeal.
- **Level 3:** The Office of Medicare Hearings and Appeals (OMHA) reviews the appeal. The amount of the case must be at least $180.
- **Level 4:** The Medicare Appeals Council reviews the appeal.

- **Level 5:** This is a judicial review by a federal district court. The claim amount must be at least $1,840.

How can a person win a Medicare appeal?

It is the responsibility of individuals to submit as much supporting material as they can with their appeal. An individual may be able to make positive decisions with the assistance of information obtained from doctors, other medical experts, or suppliers.

Fast appeal

If waiting for a ruling will hurt a person's health, they have the option of requesting a speedy appeal. One scenario that illustrates the need to make a choice quickly is when an individual is an inpatient at a hospital or skilled nursing facility (SNF) and they are concerned that the facility is releasing them too soon. The Beneficiary and Family Centered Care-Quality Improvement Organization (BFCC-QIO) has the authority to conduct an instant evaluation that the individual is entitled to if this occurs. The announcement contains information on how to get in touch. During the time that the BFCC-QIO is evaluating the case, the hospital is unable to discharge the individual, and they are permitted to remain in the hospital at no further cost. The BFCC-QIO has a period of seventy-two hours to decide the appeal. At least two days before the coverage expires, a notice will be sent to an individual who is currently residing in a nursing facility or another inpatient setting. After the close of business on the day before an individual is scheduled to be freed, the BFCC-QIO has until the end of the business day to decide the appeal.

Time limits to an appeal

Depending on the Medicare part, the time limits for appeals are different. An individual has a period of one hundred and twenty days from the day they got the notice to file an appeal for Original Medicare (parts A and B). When it comes to Medicare Advantage plans and Part D prescription drug coverage, an individual has sixty days from the day they got the notification to file an appeal.

Canceling an appeal

If a person wishes to cancel their appeal to Medicare, they are required to contact Medicare at the following number: 800-MEDICARE (800-633-4227). **Specifically, they will be required to supply the following information:**
- Their full name
- Their Medicare ID number
- The date they submitted the appeal form
- Details about the appeal
- The reason they are canceling the appeal

Costs to appeal

The appeals procedure for Medicare does not incur any charges throughout the appeals process. At the State Health Insurance Assistance Program in their area, individuals can receive free assistance with the appeals process as well as assistance with any other Medicare-related issue.

Tips for Resolving Issues with Medicare

The process of navigating Medicare may be difficult at times, particularly when problems such as denied claims, uncertainty about eligibility, or billing mistakes occur. To effectively resolve these difficulties, it is necessary to have a solid awareness of the regulations and processes that govern Medicare, as well as to be aware of the appropriate actions to take and the best places to seek assistance. The following are some of the most important strategies for addressing **typical Medicare concerns, including claims that have been refused, arguments over coverage, billing issues, and locating the appropriate information.**

1. **Understand Your Medicare Coverage**

Acquiring a comprehensive understanding of your Medicare coverage is the initial step in resolving any problem that may arise with the program. The Medicare program is broken up into various sections, each of which has its own set of regulations and coverage areas:

Medicare Part A (Hospital Insurance): Covers inpatient hospital care, skilled nursing facility care, hospice, and some home health services.

Medicare Part B (Medical Insurance): Covers outpatient care, doctor visits, preventive services, and medical equipment.

Medicare Part C (Medicare Advantage): An alternative to Original Medicare, it bundles Parts A, B, and often Part D into a single plan, typically with additional benefits like dental and vision.

Medicare Part D (Prescription Drug Coverage): Covers prescription medications.

To evaluate if your problem is the result of a misunderstanding of coverage or a genuine error, it is helpful to be aware of the services or treatments that are covered by your plan as well as those that are not covered by it.

2. **Keep Detailed Records**

When you are attempting to address concerns, it is necessary to have a comprehensive record of your medical care, claims, and communications with Medicare or healthcare providers. Make sure you keep copies of the following:

Medicare Summary Notices (MSN): The Medicare Summary Notices (MSN) are statements that are sent quarterly and include information on the expenditures that Medicare has paid for as well as the charges that you may be accountable for. It is important to check these frequently.

Explanation of Benefits (EOB): If you are enrolled in a Medicare Advantage plan or Medicare Part D, your plan will give you an EOB that explains the services or drugs that were covered and the reasons for their coverage.

Receipts and Bills: Save all your receipts and itemized invoices from your healthcare providers. This means you should save all of your bills. You will be able to cross-check what was invoiced and what Medicare has paid with the assistance of these records.

Communication Log: Keep a record of any phone conversations or written correspondence you have with Medicare, your insurance plan, or your healthcare provider. This is necessary to comply with the requirements of the Communication Log. The date of the call, the name of the representative, and the topics that were addressed should all be written down.

3. Resolve Billing Errors

Billing concerns are among the most often encountered concerns that Medicare recipients struggle with. Resolving billing issues as promptly as possible will help you avoid incurring unneeded out-of-pocket costs. This is true whether the service in question was invoiced wrongly or the amount that you owe was calculated incorrectly. I will tell you what you can do:

Review Your Medicare Summary Notice (MSN) or Explanation of Benefits (EOB): Carefully examine your statement to identify any inconsistencies, such as services that you did not get or inaccurate amounts that were charged to your account.

Contact the Provider First: If you discover a problem in the billing, you should get in touch with the healthcare provider that issued the charge. They could have billed Medicare or your Medicare Advantage plan incorrectly. This might have been a mistake on their part. You should request that they recheck the claim and resubmit it if it is required.

Contact Medicare or Your Insurance Plan: If the provider is unable to fix the issue, you should get in touch with Medicare (for Original Medicare claims) or your Medicare Advantage or Part D plan to inquire about the amount. To clarify the situation, you should be ready to supply precise facts from your MSN or EOB records.

4. Appeal a Denied Claim

It is within your rights to file an appeal if Medicare or your Medicare Advantage or Part D plan does not provide coverage for a particular treatment. To approach the procedure in the following manner:

Understand the Reason for Denial: It is important to read either your Medicare Summary Notice (MSN) or your Explanation of Benefits (EOB) to have an understanding of the reason why the treatment was refused. There might be a lack of medical need or the service might not have been covered by your plan, both of which could be the cause.

Gather Supporting Documentation: To provide documentation in support of your appeal, you should get a letter from your physician stating why the service is medically essential and include pertinent medical documents.

File an Appeal: If you are enrolled in Original Medicare, you are required to submit a request to Medicare for a redetermination within one hundred twenty days after receiving the notice of rejection. When it comes to Medicare Advantage or Part D, you should adhere to the appeals procedure that your plan has established. This process normally begins with submitting an appeal directly to the plan within sixty days of getting the rejection.

5. **Use the Medicare Appeals Process**

There are many levels of review available through Medicare's appeals procedure if your claim is refused. If your appeal is denied at one level, you have the option of taking it to the next level. **These are the levels:**

- **Redetermination:** A review of the denied claim by the Medicare contractor or your plan.
- **Reconsideration:** A second review by an independent contractor.
- **Administrative Law Judge Hearing:** If the amount in question is at least $200, you can request a hearing.
- **Medicare Appeals Council:** A review of the Administrative Law Judge's decision.
- **Judicial Review:** If the amount in dispute is over $2,000, you can request a review in federal court.

Ensure you submit your appeal promptly because there are stringent deadlines for each stage of appeal.

6. **Check for Prior Authorization or Coverage Restrictions**

Certain services provided by Medicare, particularly those provided by Medicare Advantage or Medicare Part D, need prior permission. Additionally, certain Medicare services may be subject to coverage restrictions, such as step therapy or quantity limits for prescription medicines. If you are subject to these limitations, follow these steps:

Request Prior Authorization: Together with your physician, you should submit a request for priority authorization. This request provides an explanation as to why the service or medicine is required for medical reasons.

Request an Exception: If your health insurance plan imposes limitations on a certain prescription or therapy, you should consult with your physician to obtain an exemption. If you can demonstrate that there are no other therapies or medications that would be effective for your illness, then you may be given an exception.

Use Expedited Appeals: If the rejection of a service or medicine poses an immediate threat to your health, you have the option of submitting a request for an expedited appeal, which must be processed within three days.

7. **Take Advantage of Free Medicare Counseling Services**

State Health Insurance Assistance Program, sometimes known as SHIP, is a program that is offered at no cost to those who are beneficiaries of Medicare. Helping you understand your Medicare coverage, resolving billing difficulties, and navigating the appeals process are all things that SHIP counselors may assist you with. They can provide individualized help and provide objective counsel.

On the website of the SHIP National Technical Assistance Center, you may find the contact information for your local SHIP office. Alternatively, you can call Medicare at 1-800-MEDICARE (1-800-633-4227) to receive a referral.

8. **Contact Medicare for Assistance**

If you have attempted to resolve a problem with your Medicare plan or provider without any success, you have the option of contacting Medicare directly:

Call 1-800-MEDICARE (1-800-633-4227): You can speak with a Medicare person by calling 1-800-MEDICARE (1-800-633-4227). This representative will be able to assist you in resolving claims difficulties, explaining your benefits, and guiding you through the appeals process.

Visit Medicare.gov: Detailed information about Medicare coverage, claims, and the appeals process may be found on the official Medicare website, which can be accessed by visiting Medicare.gov. Additionally, you can monitor the progress of your claims by logging onto your MyMedicare.gov account.

9. **Know Your Rights and Protections**

You, as a beneficiary of Medicare, are entitled to certain rights that safeguard you when dealing with Medicare-related difficulties. Included in these rights are:

The Right to Appeal: You have the right to appeal any decision that rejects coverage or payment for a service that you feel must be covered by Medicare. This right applies to any decision that you believe should be covered by Medicare.

The Right to Timely Information: You have the right to receive information that is both clear and timely on the services that Medicare covers and the charges that you may be responsible for.

The Right to Quality Care: You have the right to get medical attention from medical professionals who are not only respectful of your wishes but also deliver care of the highest possible standard.

10. **Prevent Future Medicare Issues**

Taking these preventative measures will help you avoid problems with Medicare in the future:

Ask Questions: Before obtaining any kind of medical care, it is always a good idea to inquire from your physician about whether or not the service is covered by Medicare and whether or not there will be any out-of-pocket expenses.

Check Your Medicare Plan: If you have a Medicare Advantage or Part D plan, evaluate the coverage and network of your plan every year, particularly during the yearly Enrollment Period (which runs from October 15 to December 7), to ensure that it continues to fulfill your requirements.

Keep Your Information Up-to-Date: Ensure your personal information, such as address and contact details, is up to date with Medicare and your healthcare providers.

CHAPTER 9
MEDICARE AND LONG-TERM CARE
What Medicare Covers for Long-Term Care

The costs of long-term medical care, assisted living, and nursing homes have gone up a lot in the last few decades. Genworth says that the average cost of a private room in a nursing home is now more than $100,000 per year. And even though assisted living homes are a bit less expensive, they still charge over $50,000 a year on average. Even in-home care services, which are often thought to be cheaper, can use up savings quickly. Because these costs could be so high, it's important to start planning for long-term care long before you retire. However, a lot of people think that Medicare will cover them because they depend on it to pay for their medical bills after they stop working. Indeed, these programs are very important because they cover a wide range of medical needs, from regular check-ups to hospital stays and prescription drugs, making it much easier for people to pay for many medical services. Medicare can be very helpful for retired people, but it was made to cover urgent medical needs and short-term care, not the kind of long-term help that is often needed for long-term care. This brings up an important question: How much does Medicare pay for long-term care?

What long-term care costs does Medicare cover?

Medicare doesn't cover a lot of the costs of long-term care. When it comes to long-term care, Medicare covers the following:

Skilled nursing facility care

Medicare Part A will pay for care in a skilled nursing home, but only in certain situations and for a certain amount of time. To be eligible, you must have been in the hospital for at least three days and need skilled care connected to that stay. For every 100 days of service, there is full coverage for the first 20 days and half coverage for days 21 through 100.

Home health care

While you're at home, Medicare will pay for some skilled nursing care, physical therapy, occupational therapy, and other skilled care services if you meet certain requirements. This coverage is usually only for a short time, though, and it doesn't cover 24-hour care, food delivery, or help with daily tasks like bathing and dressing.

Hospice care

Medicare covers all hospice care for people with fatal illnesses. This includes medical care, prescription drugs to ease symptoms, and support services for patients and their families.

Hospital stays

Medicare covers hospital stays, which aren't usually thought of as long-term care but can be longer in cases of serious sickness or accident. **It is important to know that Medicare does not pay for:**
- Custodial care (help with activities of daily living) when that's the only care needed
- Long-term care in assisted living facilities or nursing homes beyond the limited skilled nursing facility coverage mentioned above
- Non-medical home care services

How to cover the costs of long-term care

The problems listed above mean that most people shouldn't depend on Medicare alone for long-term care needs. Instead, you might want to think about these other options:

Long-term care insurance

Getting the right long-term care insurance coverage is often the best way to cover the costs of long-term care. Long-term care insurance is meant to cover the costs of long-term care needs, such as assisted living, nursing home care, and home care services.
Most of the time, these plans will offer:
- **Comprehensive coverage:** Policies can be tailored to cover a lot of different types of care, so you can pick the kind of care you get.
- **Asset protection:** Long-term care insurance helps you keep your savings and other assets for other uses or to leave to your children or grandchildren.
- **Customization options:** You can pick the amount of coverage, the length of the benefits, and other features that work best for your wants and budget.
- **Tax advantages:** Some premiums may be tax-deductible, and most benefits are not taxed when they are received.

Medicare supplemental coverage

You can also get Medicare supplement insurance to help pay for some long-term care costs. For instance, if you have this kind of coverage, it might pay for your daily share if you stay in a skilled nursing facility for up to 100 days. This lowers the amount of money you have to pay out of pocket for short-term treatment or skilled nursing care. There are, however, some things that should be kept in mind. Medicare supplement plans don't cover long stays in nursing homes, assisted living facilities, or long-term home health care. That's because these plans are meant to fill in the gaps in Medicare benefits, not give full long-term care support. Specialized long-term care insurance coverage would be better for full protection during long-term care. But in some situations, your Medicare supplement plan might be able to help pay for some or all of the costs of this kind of care.

Savings and investments

Building a fund for long-term care costs through regular savings and smart investments can help cover future costs. This method needs focus and planning ahead, but it gives you options for how to spend your money.

Health savings accounts

If you qualify, putting money into a health savings account (HSA) while you're still working can help you save money on taxes while planning for future medical costs, such as some long-term care costs.

Medicaid

Medicaid can cover more of your long-term care costs if you meet certain income and wealth standards. But this choice is usually only for seniors with low incomes because you have to spend down your assets to qualify. This means that people who have a lot of money saved for retirement or assets won't be able to use it.

Alternatives for Long-Term Care (Medicaid, Private Insurance)

Medicare only covers a certain amount of long-term care, so people who need long-term nursing home care, in-home help, or other types of support must look into other options. Medicaid, private long-term care insurance, and several personal and family resources are common ways to pay for long-term care. **Take a look at these other options and how they can help you pay for long-term care:**

1. **Medicaid**

Medicaid is a program run by both the federal government and the states. It helps people with low incomes get health insurance and pays for long-term care services. It is one of the most important ways that people in the United States can get money for long-term care.

Medicaid Eligibility for Long-Term Care

People must meet certain income and wealth limits to get Medicaid long-term care payments.

Rules for getting Medicaid change from state to state, but in most cases, a person must have very little income and almost no assets (in most states, no more than $2,000 in assets can be counted).

- **Income Limits:** Each state has its own rules about how much money someone can make, but in many states, the income level needed to qualify for care in a nursing home or at home is lower than a certain amount.
- **Asset Limits:** Most of your assets may be counted toward Medicaid eligibility, but your main home (up to a certain value limit), your car, and some of your items may not be. A lot of people spend their assets as part of their Medicaid plans to meet the standards for getting Medicaid.
- **Spousal Protections:** If only one partner needs long-term care, Medicaid rules let the healthy spouse (also called the community spouse) keep a certain amount of money and property. This keeps the healthy spouse from going broke because of the cost of caring for the sick partner.

Types of Long-Term Care Medicaid Covers

Medicaid covers a lot of different types of long-term care, such as:

- **Nursing Home Care:** If you need nursing home care for medical reasons and can prove you can afford it, Medicaid will pay for it.
- **Home and Community-Based Services (HCBS):** Many states have Medicaid waiver programs that let people who qualify get care at home or in the community instead of in a nursing home. Home health workers, help with daily tasks, and adult day care services are some of these services.

Pros and Cons of Medicaid

Pros

- Offers full coverage for long-term care to people who apply.
- Waiver programs pay for both nursing home care and activities that can be done in the home.
- Spousal protections laws help keep the healthy spouse from becoming poor.

Cons

- Because of strict limits on income and assets, you may need to do a lot of financial planning to be eligible.
- There may be long wait times in some states for Medicaid waivers that cover home-based care.
- Not all care homes will take Medicaid people, so there aren't many options.
2. **Private Long-Term Care Insurance**

Long-term care insurance is a type of private insurance that can help pay for long-term care services. People usually buy this insurance a long time before they need care, and it can cover care at home, in an assisted living facility, at an adult day care, or in a nursing home.

How Long-Term Care Insurance Works

- **Premiums:** You have to pay premiums for long-term care insurance every month or once a year. The amount of coverage you choose, your health, and your age at the time of buying are some of the things that affect how much your rates are.
- **Coverage:** Long-term care insurance plans cover different types of care, but most of them offer a daily benefit amount for services like in-home care, adult day care, assisted living, or nursing home care. Policies usually say how many years they will pay for services or how much they will pay in total throughout a person's life.
- **Waiting Period:** A lot of plans have a cooling off time or waiting period, where you have to pay for services yourself before the insurance starts to cover them. This period is usually 30 to 90 days.

Pros and Cons of Long-Term Care Insurance

Pros

- Helps pay for the high cost of long-term care services so that personal assets are not lost.
- Gives people more choices and freedom when it comes to nursing homes, assisted living, and care at home.
- It can be bought on its own or as part of combination coverage that includes life insurance or annuities.

Cons

- Premiums can be pricey, especially if you buy them later in life.
- Some policies may not cover the full cost of long-term care and have waiting times and limits on what they will pay for.
- Insurance companies can refuse to cover you if you have a pre-existing disease or are too old.

Hybrid Long-Term Care Insurance

Long-term care insurance that is combined with life insurance or pensions is called a hybrid policy. If you don't need long-term care, when you die, your family may get a life insurance refund or a pension payment.

People who want to make sure their rates aren't wasted if they never need long-term care may like this choice.

3. **Personal and Family Resources**

Along with Medicaid and long-term care insurance, a lot of people pay for long-term care with their funds, help from family, or other clever ways to get money.

Personal Savings and Retirement Funds

Many people pay for long-term care with their savings, stocks, or retirement plans like 401(k)s or IRAs. This might be possible for people with a lot of money, but the costs of long-term care can quickly wipe out funds.

Reverse Mortgages

With a reverse mortgage, people aged 62 and up can borrow against the value of their home without having to sell it. The loan doesn't have to be paid back until the owner dies, moves out, or sells the house. Backward mortgage money can be used to pay for long-term care services like in-home care.

Pros

- Let's you stay in your own home and get money for care.
- There are no monthly mortgage payments to make.

Cons

- Lowers the value of your estate because the loan has to be paid back when you die or when you sell your home.
- Reverse mortgages come with a lot of complicated rules and high fees.

Life Insurance Policy Conversion

Some types of life insurance let owners get the money from their coverage while they are still living. This is called accelerated death benefits or life settlements. It's possible to pay for long-term care with the money.

Pros

- It gives you a way to pay for care, while keeping your life insurance benefits.

Cons

- When you use your life insurance early, the reward that goes to the policyholder's beneficiaries is lessened.

Annuities

Some people buy delayed annuities, which give them a steady income in retirement that they can use to pay for long-term care. There are also long-term care annuities, which cover both the regular payouts of an annuity and the costs of long-term care.

Pros

- Gives a steady flow of money for life, which can help pay for long-term care costs.

Cons

- Needs a big starting investment.
- Depending on how much the pension pays out, it might not cover the full cost of care.
4. **Community and Nonprofit Programs**

There is also neighborhood and charity groups that can help lower the cost of long-term care, especially for people who want to stay at home while getting care.

PACE (Program of All-Inclusive Care for the Elderly): PACE, or the Program of All-Inclusive Care for the Elderly, helps older people get care in their own homes or neighborhoods instead of nursing homes. It is a Medicare and Medicaid program. PACE offers medical care, social services, and help with daily tasks.

Veterans' Benefits: The U.S. Department of Veterans Affairs (VA) helps soldiers get long-term care, such as in-home care, nursing home care, and adult day care. Service experience, income, and physical needs are used to decide who is eligible.

Local Senior Services: Many towns and cities have programs through senior centers, groups, or the government that help older people stay in their own homes by providing in-home care, meal delivery, transportation, and other services.

Nursing Homes and In-Home Care: Coverage Limits

In-home care and care in a nursing home are two of the most popular types of long-term care. It is important to know how Medicare and other financial programs cover these services, as well as the limits of each, to make plans. Medicare only covers a small amount of both types of care, focusing mostly on short-term, medically necessary care rather than long-term care that keep someone locked up. For long-term care, people usually need to look into other choices, such as Medicaid, private insurance, or their own money.

1. **Nursing Home Care Coverage Limits Under Medicare**

Medicare will only pay for certain kinds of skilled nursing care in a nursing home or rehab center. This is not the same as long-term residential care, which people who can't do daily tasks on their own often need.

When Medicare Covers Nursing Home Care

- **Post-Hospitalization:** When someone has been to the hospital for at least three days, which is calculated as three midnights in a row, Medicare will pay for their care in a skilled nursing facility (SNF).
- **Medically Necessary Skilled Care:** The care must be medically necessary and given by skilled workers, like registered nurses, physical therapists, or occupational therapists. Some examples are taking care of wounds, physical treatment, and giving shots through an IV.

Medicare's Coverage of Skilled Nursing Facility Care

- **First 20 Days:** If you meet the standards, Medicare Part A will pay for all of your costs in a skilled nursing home for the first 20 days.
- **Days 21–100:** You have to pay a daily payment to Medicare for days 21 through 100. The share is $200 per day in 2024.
- **After 100 Days:** Medicare coverage stops after 100 days in a skilled nursing home for each benefit period. After this point, the patient is in charge of paying for all of their care.

What Medicare Does Not Cover

- **Custodial Care:** Medicare does not cover custodial care, which includes help with things like bathing, dressing, eating, and going to the bathroom. People who are getting older, disabled, or have a long-term illness but don't need skilled medical care usually need this kind of long-term care.
- **Permanent Residency in Nursing Homes:** Medicare doesn't pay for long-term living in a nursing home if it's mostly for guardianship care.

2. **In-Home Care Coverage Limits Under Medicare**

Medicare does pay for some in-home care, but only for skilled care services that are medically required.

Medicare-Covered Home Health Care

If you meet certain criteria, Medicare Part A and/or Part B may pay for some home health services.

Eligibility Requirements

- You must be considered **homebound**, meaning it is difficult for you to leave your home without assistance.
- A doctor must certify that you need intermittent **skilled nursing care** or **therapy services** (physical, speech, or occupational therapy).
- Care must be provided by a **Medicare-certified** home health agency.

Covered Services

- **Skilled Nursing Care:** Includes services such as administering medications, wound care, or monitoring a serious illness.
- **Therapy Services:** Medicare covers physical, occupational, and speech therapy if needed for rehabilitation after surgery or illness.
- **Home Health Aides:** Medicare may cover a **home health aide** to assist with personal care (e.g., bathing, and dressing), but only if you are also receiving skilled nursing care or therapy services.

Medicare Coverage Limits for Home Health Care

Part-Time or Intermittent Care: Home health care that is part-time or irregular is the only kind of care that Medicare will pay for (less than 8 hours per day and less than 28 hours per week). It doesn't pay for full-time care at home.

Custodial Care Not Covered: Medicare does not pay for long-term care given by a guardian in the home. Medicare won't pay for care that only helps you with ADLs.

Medical Equipment and Supplies: As long as a doctor prescribes it, Medicare will pay for durable medical equipment (DME) used in the home, like walkers, wheelchairs, and breathing equipment.

3. **Medicaid Coverage for Nursing Home and In-Home Care**

Medicare only covers a certain amount of long-term care, but Medicaid covers more, including care in a nursing home and at home for people who qualify financially.

Medicaid and Nursing Home Care

Long-term nursing home care, such as skilled nursing care and domestic care, is covered by Medicaid as long as the person meets the program's medical and financial requirements.

- **Eligibility:** Different states have different rules about how much money and assets someone can have. Most people have to spend their assets to get Medicaid.
- **Long-Term Nursing Home Coverage:** If you qualify, Medicaid will pay for your long-term nursing home care, which may include residential care. There is no 100-day cap on benefits like there is with Medicare.

Medicaid and In-Home Care

Home and Community-Based Services (HCBS) are another part of Medicaid that helps people who are qualified get care at home instead of in a nursing home.

- **Home-Based Services:** Personal care help, homemaker services, leisure care, and adult day care are some of the home-based services that Medicaid may pay for. People can get help with daily tasks like cleaning, getting dressed, and making meals through these services.
- **State Waiver Programs:** A lot of states have Medicaid waiver programs that help pay for in-home care for people who would need to go to a nursing home otherwise. These programs are different in each state, and in some places, the queue can be very long.

4. **Private Long-Term Care Insurance**

Private long-term care insurance is a choice for people who aren't eligible for Medicaid but want to plan for the possibility that they will need long-term care. A lot of different services, like nursing home care and in-home care, can be covered by private insurance.

Coverage for Nursing Home Care

- **Daily or Lifetime Benefits:** Most long-term care insurance plans pay a set amount each day for nursing home care. Depending on the policy, they will either pay for care for a set number of years (like three or five years) or for life.

Coverage for In-Home Care

- **Home Care Benefits:** A lot of long-term care insurance plans cover in-home care services like personal care help, home health workers, and skilled nursing care.
- **Flexibility:** People who get long-term care insurance can usually get care at home, in an assisted living facility, or in a nursing home, based on their choice and the amount of care they need.

Cost of Long-Term Care Insurance

- **Premiums:** The costs of your insurance rely on your age, health, and the amount of coverage you pick. Long-term care insurance fees will be less expensive if you buy it early.
- **Waiting Periods:** Before your insurance starts to pay for services, you usually have to pay for them out of your pocket during a waiting period, which is also known as an elimination period.

5. **Personal and Family Resources for Paying for Long-Term Care**

Many people pay for long-term care services out of their savings or with help from family members when they don't have Medicaid or private insurance.

Out-of-Pocket Payment

Paying for nursing home or in-home care out of pocket is a choice for people who have a lot of money. Long-term care, on the other hand, can be very pricey. Nursing home costs range from $7,000 to $10,000 per month, based on where the facility is located and the type of care it offers.

Reverse Mortgages

With a reverse mortgage, people can use the wealth in their home to pay for long-term care. This choice could be good for people who need money to pay for in-home care services but still want to get care at home.

Family Caregiving

A lot of families take care of their old relatives in their own homes, either for free or by hiring workers to help. Some states have programs that help family workers with money.

Planning for Long-Term Care Expenses

It's important to think about long-term care planning when it comes to money as we get older since most people will need help with daily tasks or medical care at some point. You can get long-term care in a nursing home or an assisted living center. This type of care helps people with their daily tasks like bathing, dressing, eating, and moving around. It also includes medical care. Because this kind of care can be very expensive, it's important to have a plan for how to pay for it. Finding out how much long-term care might cost is one of the first things that people do when they are planning for it. Long-term care is pricey. Depending on where you live and how much care you need, nursing home care can cost anywhere from $7,000 to $10,000 per month. Even though in-home care is more convenient, it can get expensive if you need workers every day. People will need to look into other ways to pay for their long-term care because Medicare doesn't cover a lot of it.

Usually, it only covers short-term skilled nursing or therapy services. Long-term care costs can be paid for by Medicaid, but people must meet tight income and asset standards to be eligible. A lot of people will have to spend down their assets to qualify. Long-term care insurance is a good choice for people who don't meet the requirements for Medicaid. It covers things like care at home, assisted living, and care in a nursing home. It can help keep your savings from going down the drain because of care costs. The important thing is to buy insurance as soon as possible because prices go up with age and some health problems can make it hard to qualify later on. There are other ways to get your finances ready if you can't get long-term care insurance. Some people might think about using their savings, like retirement accounts, to pay for care. People who own their own homes can use the wealth in their homes to pay for care at home through a reverse mortgage. Some people may look into using accelerated death benefits or life payments to turn their life insurance plans into cash. These funds can help pay for care costs without having to sell anything. When planning for long-term care, family help is another thing to think about. A lot of families take care of elderly relatives, either by doing it for free or by sharing their money to hire professional help. Sometimes, states help family members financially or give them tax breaks, which can make things easier. To sum up, making plans for long-term care costs needs a thorough approach that considers personal finances, possible insurance choices, and state programs such as Medicaid. People can protect their assets and make sure they have the money they need for long-term care when they need it by thinking about these things early on.

CHAPTER 10

MEDICARE FRAUD AND ABUSE PREVENTION

Common Types of Medicare Fraud

Medicare fraud is a big problem that costs billions of dollars every year in wrong payouts and hurts both recipients and the healthcare system as a whole. Medicare fraud usually happens when healthcare workers, suppliers, or even beneficiaries file false claims to get paid for services or supplies that were not given or were not needed. Knowing the most common types of Medicare scams can help you stay safe and report any behavior that seems fishy.

1. **Billing for Services or Supplies Not Provided**

Providers who bill Medicare for services, treatments, or medical products that were never given to the patient are one of the most common types of Medicare fraud. A doctor could bill Medicare for a test or surgery that the patient never got, or a supplier could charge for long-term medical tools like wheelchairs or walkers that were never sent.

2. **Upcoding**

When healthcare workers bill Medicare for a more expensive service or treatment than what was done, this is called upcoding. For example, a provider might do an easy treatment but bill Medicare for a more complicated and expensive one so that they can get more money back.

3. **Unnecessary Services or Procedures**

Some doctors cheat their patients by giving them services, tests, or treatments that they don't need and then paying for them. These services are only done to get Medicare payments, so they are not needed. As an example, a doctor might ask for scans or lab tests that aren't needed for the patient's situation.

4. **Kickbacks and Bribes**

Providers sometimes take part in kickback scams, in which they get paid money or gifts for sending patients to certain medical services or providers or sellers. These payments can cause Medicare to pay for services that aren't needed or aren't right for the patient.

5. **Identity Theft**

Personal information about Medicare recipients, such as their Medicare cards, is sometimes stolen or used by people or groups to falsely bill Medicare for services or goods. This can happen if a provider files claims for services that a patient never got using information about a recipient.

6. **Billing for Services Performed by Unqualified Personnel**

Billing Medicare for services that were done by people who aren't licensed or qualified is another type of theft. For example, medical aids doing work that should only be done by a licensed doctor is an example of this. After that, the services are billed as if they were done by a qualified medical worker.

7. **False Cost Reports**

Medicare fraud can also happen in institutions like hospitals and nursing homes, where workers report fake or inflated costs to get more money from Medicare. The purpose of these cost reports is to show how much the services cost, but false reports can make bills look higher than they are.

How to Protect Yourself from Medicare Fraud

- **Review Your Medicare Summary Notice (MSN) or Explanation of Benefits (EOB):** You should do this regularly to make sure that all the services mentioned are correct and match the care you got.
- **Protect Your Medicare Number:** Think of your Medicare card and number like a credit card. Do not give it to anyone other than your doctor or someone you trust.
- **Report Suspicious Activity:** If you see any services or charges on your MSN or EOB that don't make sense, aren't familiar, or aren't right, you should call 1-800-MEDICARE or your Medicare plan provider to report what might be fraud.

How to Detect and Report Fraud

To find Medicare fraud, you need to pay close attention to the services and treatments you get and the paperwork you get from Medicare. **Here are some important things you can do to spot possible fraud:**

1. **Review Your Medicare Summary Notice (MSN) or Explanation of Benefits (EOB)**

If you have Original Medicare, Medicare will send you a Medicare Summary Notice (MSN). If you have a Medicare Advantage or Part D plan, Medicare will send you an Explanation of Benefits (EOB). The services and things that were billed to Medicare and the amounts that were paid for you are shown in these papers. Carefully read these letters to find any charges that don't seem right or aren't known.

Watch out for these signs of fraud

- **Unfamiliar Services or Items:** Check for services, procedures, or medical equipment that you didn't receive.
- **Duplicate Charges:** Watch out for multiple charges for the same service or item.
- **Unnecessary Services:** Be wary of services that seem excessive or medically unnecessary.
- **Incorrect Dates:** Verify that the dates of service match when you received care.

2. **Keep a Personal Health Care Journal**

Keep track of all of your doctor visits, tests, treatments, and any medical supplies or medicines you get. Check this log against your MSN or EOB to make sure that everything written here fits the services and things you were given. This can help you find any mistakes or claims that are not true.

3. **Be Cautious with Your Medicare Number**

If someone steals your Medicare card and uses it to make fake claims that is fraud. Like a credit card, you should keep your Medicare card and number safe. Never give them to anyone else, not your healthcare providers, over the phone, online, or in person. Watch out for people who offer free medical care or supplies in return for your Medicare number. A lot of the time, this is how theft is done.

4. **Question Unnecessary or Excessive Services**

If your doctor wants you to go through too many tests or treatments that don't seem to be connected to your situation, you should ask them why. Before you go ahead with a service, make sure you know why you need it. Fraudulent doctors may do services that aren't needed just to get Medicare to pay for them.

How to Report Medicare Fraud

It is very important to report Medicare theft right away if you think it is happening. Here's how to report theft that you think it is:

1. **Contact Medicare**

You can tell Medicare directly that you think someone is committing fraud by calling:

- **1-800-MEDICARE (1-800-633-4227)**
- **TTY users:** 1-877-486-2048

When you report, make sure you have these things ready:

- Your name and Medicare number
- The name of the provider or supplier involved
- The service or item you're questioning
- The date of the service
- Why do you believe it's a fraud (e.g., services you didn't receive, duplicate billing)

Medicare will look into your report and do what needs to be done.

2. **Contact the Office of Inspector General (OIG)**

You can also tell the Office of Inspector General (OIG) about Medicare theft. The OIG looks into Medicare fraud, waste, and abuse. This is what can be done:

- **Online:** At the OIG website (https://oig.hhs.gov)
- **By phone:** Call the OIG hotline at 1-800-HHS-TIPS (1-800-447-8477)
- **By mail:** Download a complaint form from the OIG website, fill it out, and mail it to the OIG.

You can stay private when you report something to the OIG, but giving your contact information will help agents get in touch with you if they need more information.

3. **Contact Your Medicare Advantage or Part D Plan**

If you have a Medicare Advantage or Part D plan, you can tell your plan provider about theft immediately. There must be a way for each plan to handle scam reports. Check the website for your plan or call their customer service to report anything that seems fishy.

What Happens After You Report Fraud

Medicare or the OIG will look into the matter after you report what you think is fraud. It could take a while for the review to finish, but if you gave your contact information, you will be told. If fraud is proven, Medicare may take back any money it paid to the dishonest service and take civil action against those involved. In some cases, if the problem is fixed in your favor, you may get a new bill or see changes to your Medicare Summary Notice.

Protecting Your Medicare Information

To protect your name and stop fraud, it's important to keep your Medicare details safe. Your Medicare number is just as important as your credit card or Social Security number. If it gets stolen, it could be used to commit scams that could affect your coverage and cause you to be charged for things you didn't need. Being careful with your Medicare card is one of the best ways to keep your Medicare information safe. Keep it somewhere safe, and only bring it with you when you need to see a doctor or nurse. Don't give out your Medicare number over the phone, online, or to anyone who isn't directly involved in your care. People who are trying to steal your personal information will often offer free services, medical tools, or even gifts if you give them your Medicare number. Know this: Medicare reps will never call you and ask for personal information unless you ask them to. Another important way to keep your information safe is to look over your Medicare papers regularly. Should you have Original Medicare, Medicare will send you a Medicare Summary Notice (MSN). If you have a Medicare Advantage or Part D plan, Medicare will send you an Explanation of Benefits (EOB). These lists show the things and services that were charged to Medicare on your account. By reading these comments very carefully, you can find any charges that don't make sense or seem odd. If you see charges for services you didn't get or double charges for the same service, you should call Medicare or your plan provider right away to report the problem.

You should be careful about how you share private data. Keep your information safe when you visit a healthcare provider or center. Make sure that no one can hear you or find it in a place where other people can see it. Make sure the websites you use to deal with companies or sellers are safe and real before you enter any personal information. Tell 1-800-MEDICARE or the Office of Inspector General right away if you think your Medicare information has been stolen or used in a bad way. Quick action can stop your information from being used in other ways and help protect your Medicare benefits. You can keep your Medicare information safe from scams and abuse by being careful and proactive. This will help keep your benefits safe.

CHAPTER 11
RESOURCES FOR MEDICARE BENEFICIARIES
State Health Insurance Assistance Programs (SHIPs)

State Health Insurance Assistance Programs, or SHIPs, are free therapy services that help Medicare recipients in a way that fits their needs. SHIPs help people understand their Medicare benefits and coverage choices. They also help people with problems like claims, rejections, and decisions about enrollment. They help people who need help making decisions about Medicare by giving them free information and direction. All fifty states have their SHIP. The federal government pays for them with funds from the U.S. Management for Living in Communities. Most of the time, local Area Agencies on Aging or other government agencies run these programs at the state level. SHIP counselors are trained to help people with a wide range of Medicare issues one-on-one.

Key Services Provided by SHIPs

SHIPs offer a lot of different services to help Medicare recipients make smart choices about their health care. SHIPs can help in the following ways:

- **Medicare Coverage Options:** SHIP aides can go over the specifics of Medicare Parts A, B, C (Medicare Advantage), D (Prescription Drug Coverage), and Medigap (Medicare Supplement Insurance). They explain how these plans work and help you choose the one that might fit your wants and price the best.
- **Medicare Enrollment:** If you are turning 65, SHIP counselors can help you through the process of signing up for Medicare. They can tell you when and how to sign up, as well as what fees you might face if you wait too long. They can also help with special registration times for people who are leaving coverage through their job.

- **Financial Assistance Programs:** SHIPs can help you find and apply for programs like Medicaid, Medicare Savings Programs, and Extra Help for prescription drug costs that can help with Medicare costs.
- **Claims and Billing Issues:** If you've had problems with Medicare, like payment problems, rejected claims, or other issues, SHIP counselors can help you understand your rights and fix these issues.
- **Long-Term Care Options:** SHIP counselors can talk about long-term care coverage choices, such as nursing home care, in-home care, and other types of help, as well as how Medicaid and other programs can help pay for these costs.

How to Access SHIP Services

In every state, SHIP services are offered, and you can get in touch with your local office by phone, in person, or online. You can call 1-800-MEDICARE (1-800-633-4227) or go to the SHIP National Technical Assistance Center website to find the SHIP in your area. They will then connect you with your state's SHIP. SHIP services are free, and the advisers are not connected with any insurance companies, so you will get advice that isn't slanted. These services are especially helpful for Medicare recipients who are new to the program or who need help understanding complicated Medicare problems, such as their rights under the program, coverage choices, and out-of-pocket costs.

Online Tools and Resources (Medicare.gov)

Medicare.gov is the official website for Medicare in the United States. It has many online tools and services that can help Medicare recipients handle their health care, find providers, learn about their plan options, and make smart choices. The website has a lot of tools to help you, whether you are signing up for Medicare for the first time or need to make changes to your current plan. **In no particular order, these are the best Medicare.gov tools and services.**

1. **Medicare Plan Finder**

One of the most useful tools on the site is the Medicare Plan Finder. It helps people who are eligible for Medicare compare different Medicare plans, such as Medicare Advantage (Part C), Prescription Drug Plans (Part D), and Medigap (Supplemental Insurance).

It lets you find a Medicare plan for:

- Type in the names of your prescription drugs to find the cheapest plan that covers them.
- Look at the out-of-pocket costs, deductibles, and plan fees of different plans.
- Look at the star ratings for Medicare Part D and Advantage plans to get an idea of how good the coverage is.
- Look for ideas in your area and compare them side by side.

People with Medicare can change their plans for the next year during the Open Enrollment Period, which runs from October 15 to December 7. This tool is especially useful during this time.

2. **MyMedicare.gov Account**

Medicare recipients can get specific information about their benefits, claims, and payments by making an account on MyMedicare.gov. **After logging in, you can:**

- Look at your Medicare Summary Notice (MSN). It lists the services that Medicare paid for.
- Keep track of your claims and check on your bills and payments.
- Keep track of your prescription drug benefits and see how much you have to pay out of pocket for medicines.
- Make changes to your account options and contact details.

Having an account on MyMedicare.gov helps you keep track of your healthcare costs and claims. This makes it easier to spot billing mistakes or scams.

3. **Find & Compare Providers**

The Find & Compare Providers tool lets you look for and compare doctors, hospitals, nursing homes, nursing homes, and home health services.

You can do the following with this tool:

- Look for doctors who take Medicare assignments and compare how their patients rate them.
- Look up hospitals and compare success measures like the number of happy patients and the number of times they are readmitted.
- Use review scores, staffing levels, and inspection records to compare nursing homes.
- You can look up home health companies to see how well they take care of their patients and provide services.

This tool helps Medicare recipients make sure they get good care from providers who can meet their needs and are paid by Medicare.

4. **Medicare Coverage Tool**

Medicare recipients can use the Medicare Coverage Tool to find out if their plan covers a certain service, item, or treatment. This is especially helpful if you want to know what medical costs you might have to pay for yourself.

You can use this tool to look for:

- **Medical tests** (e.g., lab tests, MRIs) to see if they are covered under Medicare.
- **Durable medical equipment** (e.g., walkers, wheelchairs) to check whether Medicare will pay for these items.
- **Preventive services** (e.g., flu shots, cancer screenings) to understand the coverage and frequency of these services.

This tool can help you figure out what Medicare covers and what you might have to pay for before you go ahead with medical treatment or buy equipment.

5. **Medicare & You Handbook**

You can get the **Medicare & You** handbook on Medicare.gov in both PDF and interactive web versions. This is an in-depth book with the most up-to-date information on Medicare benefits, enrollment times, coverage rules, and other topics. This handbook is changed every year to reflect any changes to Medicare rules. It gives important information to beneficiaries during the open registration time.

You can also ask for a hard copy of the guide to be sent to you by mail.

6. **Help & Support Section**

The Medicare.gov **Help & Support** section has tools to help you solve common Medicare problems and answers to commonly asked questions. This part has the following:

- Advice on how to file a claim or query a Medicare decision.
- Step-by-step instructions on how to sign up for Medicare, change plans, or make changes to your information.
- Information on how to get help from Medicare customer service and local State Health Insurance Assistance Programs (SHIPs).

This section is very helpful for Medicare recipients who want to find answers to specific questions about their benefits or get help with claims, billing, or plan changes.

7. **Medicaid and Extra Help Information**

Medicare.gov has information on extra options like Medicaid and the Extra Help program for prescription drug costs for Medicare recipients who need financial help with their Medicare costs. The website has information on who can apply for these programs and how to do so.

8. **Medicare Forms**

If you need to fill out and send in paperwork for your Medicare benefits, you can download forms from Medicare.gov and do so. Among these forms are:

- **CMS-40B** for enrolling in Medicare Part B.
- **CMS-L564** for requesting proof of group health insurance coverage when applying for Medicare.
- Other forms for appeals, claims, or making changes to your coverage.

Having these forms in one place makes it easier and more convenient to keep up with your Medicare enrollment and changes.

Contacting Medicare for Help and Support

There are several ways to get help from Medicare if you have questions about your benefits, claims, or enrollment, or need help fixing a problem. There are several ways to get in touch with Medicare to make sure you get the help you need, such as talking to an agent over the phone, looking at information online, or asking for help in person. **To get help and guidance from Medicare, follow these steps:**

1. **Call Medicare**

The best way to get help from Medicare is to call them. Medicare gives you a toll-free number where you can talk to a customer service person right away:

Medicare Toll-Free Number: 1-800-MEDICARE (1-800-633-4227)

- **TTY users:** 1-877-486-2048
- **Hours of Operation:** Available 24 hours a day, 7 days a week.

You can get help with several things when you call, such as:

- Understanding your Medicare benefits and coverage options.
- Finding out the status of a claim.
- Reporting suspected Medicare fraud.

- Help with enrollment or making changes to your plan.
- Information about premiums, billing, and appeals.

Make sure you have your Medicare number on hand when you call. It can be found on your Medicare card.

2. **Visit Medicare.gov**

Medicare.gov is the official website for Medicare. It has a lot of information and online tools that can help you handle your coverage. **The following are some of the most useful things on the website:**

- **Medicare Plan Finder:** This tool lets you compare Medicare Advantage, Part D prescription drugs, and Medigap plans in your area.
- **MyMedicare.gov Account:** Keep an eye on your claims, look at your Medicare Summary Notices (MSN), and change your details.
- **Medicare Coverage Tool:** Use this to find out if certain services or goods are covered by Medicare.
- **Help & Support Section:** Here you can find answers to frequently asked questions, download Medicare forms, and learn how to fix problems with bills or claims.

You can get to the website whenever you want because it's open 24 hours a day, seven days a week.

3. **Email Medicare**

For personal Medicare questions, Medicare does not offer direct email help. However, you can **use the contact form on Medicare.gov to ask general questions or get more information. To do this:**

- Visit **Medicare.gov** and scroll to the bottom of the homepage.
- Click on Contact Us.
- Use the form to submit your question, and a Medicare representative will respond.

For details about your account or problems with your Medicare claims or registration, you should call 1-800-MEDICARE and talk to a real person.

4. **Get Local Help: State Health Insurance Assistance Programs (SHIPs)**

State Health Insurance Assistance Programs (SHIPs) are great if you'd rather talk to someone in person or need more in-depth, one-on-one help. SHIPs offer free, individualized guidance to Medicare recipients, which can help with anything from choosing a plan to solving problems with benefits. **SHIP counselors can help with the following:**

- Medicare Part A, B, C, and D plan comparisons.
- Enrollment and eligibility questions.
- Applying for **Medicaid** or other financial assistance programs like **Extra Help** for prescription drugs.
- Medicare billing issues and appeals.

To find a SHIP office near you:

- Visit the SHIP National Technical Assistance Center website (https://www.shiphelp.org).
- Call 1-800-MEDICARE (1-800-633-4227) for a referral to a SHIP counselor near you.

5. **Mailing Medicare**

You can mail forms, requests, or other papers to the right Medicare office if you need to send them to Medicare. Medicare may give you a different address for certain problems, but this is the main address to use for claims and general questions:

Medicare Contact Center Operations PO Box 1270 Lawrence, KS 66044

When you turn in forms, don't forget to include your Medicare number and any other important paperwork. For your records, keep copies of everything you send.

6. **Report Fraud or Abuse**

As soon as you think there is Medicare fraud or abuse, you should report it. Medicare takes theft very seriously, and telling them about any strange behavior helps keep the Medicare system and its recipients safe.

Call the Medicare Fraud Hotline: 1-800-MEDICARE (1-800-633-4227) and follow the prompts for reporting fraud.

Contact the Office of Inspector General (OIG):

- **Phone:** 1-800-HHS-TIPS (1-800-447-8477)
- **Online:** You can file a report through the OIG website (https://oig.hhs.gov).

You can stay private when you report theft, but giving your contact information can help the police.

7. **Social Security and Medicare**

For some things, like signing up for Medicare or taking care of your Medicare Part B monthly payments, which are usually taken out of your Social Security income, you may need to call the Social Security Administration (SSA).

Social Security Toll-Free Number: 1-800-772-1213

- **TTY users:** 1-800-325-0778
- **Hours of Operation:** Monday through Friday, 7:00 AM to 7:00 PM.

The SSA can help with:

- Applying for Medicare Parts A and B.
- Changing your Medicare Part B premium payment method.
- Reporting changes to your personal information (e.g., name or address).

CHAPTER 12
FUTURE OF MEDICARE
Changes and Reforms to Expect

Since its start in 1965, Medicare has been one of the biggest and most important public health programs in the United States. It has helped millions of older Americans and people with disabilities get the medical care they need. However, people are still arguing about what will happen to Medicare in the future because the program is having a hard time with money, changing demographics, and changing healthcare needs. Policymakers and other interested parties are trying to figure out how to keep Medicare going in the long run while also meeting the growing needs for healthcare services, keeping costs down, and making sure everyone has access to good care. This in-depth look at the future of Medicare will cover the main problems that are causing change, possible improvements that could be put in place, and how these changes might affect people who get Medicare.

1. **Financial Sustainability and the Medicare Trust Fund**

The Medicare Hospital Insurance (HI) Trust Fund, which pays for Medicare Part A (hospital insurance), is one of the most important things to worry about when it comes to the future of Medicare. The HI Trust Fund gets most of its money from income taxes, but it has been running deficits for years because of rising healthcare costs and an older population. The Medicare Trustees' Annual Report says that the HI Trust Fund will run out of money by 2031 if policy changes are not made. For example, Medicare will not be able to cover the full cost of hospital stays. If the government doesn't find ways to bring in more money or cut costs, Medicare could face a major financial problem.

Several ways have been talked about to deal with the Medicare Trust Fund's potential shortfall:

- **Increasing Payroll Taxes:** Increasing the amount of the payroll tax that pays for Medicare could bring in more money to keep the program going. This would need to be done by the government, but it might help secure the trust fund in the short run.
- **Reducing Benefits or Payments:** Cutting Medicare benefits, especially for people with higher incomes, or payments to hospitals and doctors could help bring down the total cost of the program. Politicians might not like this choice, though, and it might affect the level of care that people who are eligible get.
- **General Revenue Funding:** Transferring more of Medicare's funding from specific payroll taxes to general tax revenue could give the program a much-needed cash boost to cover its rising costs. To do this too, government tax policies and spending goals would have to be changed.

2. **Demographic Shifts and Increased Enrollment**

The continued change in the population is another big thing that will affect the future of Medicare. The U.S. population is getting older quickly. Every day, 10,000 baby boomers turn 65 and can start getting Medicare. All baby boomers will be 65 or older by 2030, and the number of people on Medicare will rise from about 65 million in 2024 to 80 million by 2030. Medicare's resources will be put under more stress because of this big rise in users, especially when it comes to hospital and doctor services, prescription drug costs, and long-term care needs. As more people sign up for Medicare, the healthcare system will have to make sure it can meet the needs of a growing number of seniors while keeping prices low and care quality high. Healthcare providers and Medicare Advantage plans will probably need to grow their networks. They will also need to come up with new ways to manage healthcare services, especially for people who have long-term illnesses.

3. **The Shift Toward Value-Based Care**

Medicare is changing from standard fee-for-service models, in which providers are paid based on how many services they provide, to value-based care, which focuses on better patient results and cutting down on wasteful spending. In the next few years, this change is likely to speed up as lawmakers and healthcare leaders look for ways to make Medicare work better and cost less. Providers are encouraged to provide high-quality care at lower costs by value-based care models like Accountable Care Organizations (ACOs) and bundled payment programs. These models focus on care management, preventive services, and lowering hospital readmissions. The idea behind these models is to move Medicare's financial risk to providers. This should push providers to better handle care and avoid problems that cost a lot of money. Value-based care is likely to be used by more Medicare users in the future because of changes that are being considered. A value-based approach is already used by Medicare Advantage plans, and their growth is likely to continue. More people will choose these plans as an alternative to traditional Medicare.

4. **Prescription Drug Reform**

One of the fastest-growing parts of Medicare spending is on prescription drugs. This is especially true for Medicare Part D, which covers prescription drugs. Rising drug prices are a big problem for both lawmakers and people who get government benefits. This is because high out-of-pocket costs can make it hard for seniors and people with disabilities to get the medicines they need. The Inflation Reduction Act of 2022, which made several important changes to Medicare's prescription drug benefit, is one of the most important improvements in recent years.

- **Medicare Drug Price Negotiation:** Beginning in 2026, Medicare will be able to talk directly with drug companies about the prices of some very expensive prescription drugs. This should lower costs for both Medicare recipients and the Medicare program.
- **Out-of-Pocket Cap:** By 2025, Medicare Part D will put a limit on how much people will have to pay out of pocket for prescription drugs. This will lower the amount that people pay each year. This will help people who are having a hard time paying for their drugs because they are too expensive right now, especially those who have long-term illnesses that need expensive treatments.
- **Expanded Coverage for Vaccines:** More vaccines are now covered by Medicare Part D, so users don't have to pay anything out of pocket for suggested vaccines.

These changes are a big step toward keeping the costs of prescription drugs down, but more may need to be done to stop drug prices from going up. In the future, changes could be made that give Medicare more power to discuss drug prices or add more price controls to keep costs down.

5. **Telehealth Expansion and Digital Health Innovations**

After the COVID-19 pandemic, telehealth services grew quickly, letting Medicare recipients get care from the comfort of their own houses. Virtual care has been welcomed by both patients and doctors, making it easier for more people to get care, especially those who live in rural or underserved areas. As telehealth continues to become more popular, Medicare is likely to make some of the changes that were made temporarily during the pandemic permanent. **These changes include:**

- **Expanded Telehealth Coverage:** Medicare may continue to cover telehealth services for a wider range of conditions and specialties. This means that Medicare recipients can get routine care, mental health services, and even treatment for chronic diseases without having to go to the doctor's office in person.
- **Digital Health Tools:** Medicare might look into covering new digital health tools and gadgets that let people with long-term conditions be watched from afar. This includes apps, smart tech, and home tech that keep an eye on health numbers like heart rate, blood sugar, and blood pressure.

Continuing to add telehealth and digital health tools to Medicare could lower costs, improve patient results, and give beneficiaries more easy ways to get care.

6. **Addressing Long-Term Care Needs**

Long-term care, which includes help with daily tasks like bathing, dressing, and eating, is one of the main things that Medicare doesn't cover. At the moment, Medicare only covers certain types of care in skilled nursing facilities after a hospital stay or home health services. It does not cover any kind of domestic care in nursing homes or assisted living facilities. There is more and more demand to fix this Medicare coverage gap as the population ages and more people need long-term care services. **Possible changes for the future are:**

- **Medicare Long-Term Care Benefits:** Some lawmakers want to make Medicare cover a wider range of long-term care services, either through the regular Medicare program or through Medicare Advantage plans. This could help people who depend on Medicaid or their savings to pay for long-term care bills a lot with their money.
- **Integration with Medicaid:** Medicare and Medicaid could work together more closely to make it easier for recipients to switch between Medicare and Medicaid. This is because Medicaid pays for most low-income people's long-term care.

7. **Medicare Advantage Growth and Reforms**

Over the past ten years, Medicare Advantage (Part C), which lets people get Medicare benefits through private insurance plans, has grown very quickly. Medicare Advantage plans will cover almost half of all Medicare recipients in 2024, and this trend is likely to continue. Traditional Medicare doesn't cover things like eye, dental, or hearing care, but Medicare Advantage plans do. They also offer fitness programs. But Medicare Advantage plans' cost and quality are getting more and more attention. There are worries about insurers getting too much money and networks not being strong enough.

Future reforms could include:
- **Tightening Payment Models:** Medicare could change how it pays Medicare Advantage plans to make sure that payments are based on the real costs of care and to stop paying too much.
- **Ensuring Adequate Networks:** Lawmakers could make it more difficult for Medicare Advantage plans to keep their networks of providers small enough so that recipients can get the services they need.

Medicare and the Aging Population

The connection between Medicare and the US's fast-aging population is very important to the country's healthcare system. Medicare helps people 65 and older get the medical care they need, as well as younger people with challenges. As people get older, they need Medicare's services at a rate that has never been seen before. There are both challenges and chances for the program in this change. Medicare will need to make changes to make sure it can continue to provide high-quality, easily available care while staying financially stable. This piece talks about how an older population affects Medicare, the problems it causes, and the changes that might be needed in the coming years to fix these problems.

1. **Demographic Changes Driving Increased Demand**

As the baby boomer group continues to get older, there is a big change happening in the U.S. People born between 1946 and 1964 are known as baby boomers. They started turning 65 in 2011, which means they can get Medicare. As more people in this group hit retirement age, more people have signed up for Medicare. All of the baby boomers will be 65 or older by 2030. By that time, there will be over 80 million Medicare recipients, up from about 65 million in 2024. **This rise in the number of older people has caused Medicare several problems, including:**

- **Higher Healthcare Demand:** Older people usually need more medical care because of health problems that come with getting older, chronic diseases, and the need for long-term care. Because of this, there is more demand for Medicare-covered services like skilled nursing care, hospital stays, outpatient care, and prescription drugs.
- **Increased Spending:** As the population ages, more people need health care, which means Medicare spends more generally. As more people use healthcare services and live longer, the prices of hospital stays, doctor visits, prescription drugs, and long-term care are going up for Medicare.

2. **Healthcare Needs of an Aging Population**

As people get older, they are more likely to get long-term illnesses that need ongoing medical care. Older people often have long-term illnesses like diabetes, heart disease, arthritis, and Alzheimer's. To manage these conditions, they need to see their doctors often, take their medicines, and sometimes stay in the hospital or get long-term care. As people get older, they are also more likely to experience cognitive loss and diseases like Alzheimer's and dementia. These conditions raise healthcare costs and make it necessary for more specialized care services, like home health aides and nursing home care. Medicare has to work hard to make sure that older people can get the care they need, keep prices down, and improve their quality of life. Medicare is set up to cover a lot of the medical care that older people need, but there are some services that it doesn't cover, like long-term care and dental, eye, and hearing care. It's more important than ever to close these gaps as the population ages.

3. **Financial Sustainability of Medicare**

One of the biggest worries about Medicare's future is that it won't be able to keep paying its bills as people get older. The program is mostly paid for by two types of taxes: premiums and salary taxes for Medicare Part A (hospital insurance); and general tax funds and other sources for Medicare Part B (medical insurance) and Part D (prescription drug coverage). It is expected that by 2031, the Medicare Hospital Insurance Trust Fund, which pays for Medicare Part A, will be empty. If something isn't fixed, the trust fund will only be able to pay a part of hospital insurance payments after this point. In this case, there is a big problem because medical treatments are a big part of Medicare for older people. **Medicare's financial problems are caused by several things, including:**

- **Rising Healthcare Costs:** Healthcare costs have been increasing faster than the general rate of inflation, putting pressure on Medicare's budget.
- **Increased Life Expectancy:** People are living longer, meaning they rely on Medicare for more years of healthcare coverage.
- **Higher Demand for Services:** As the number of Medicare beneficiaries grows, so does the demand for medical services, including surgeries, hospitalizations, and prescription drugs.

4. **Potential Reforms to Address the Aging Population**

To deal with the problems that come with an older population, Medicare will need to be changed in ways that keep people able to get care, improve quality, and keep costs down. Several policy choices and changes are being thought about to make sure that Medicare can last for a long time:

Raising the Medicare Eligibility Age

Some people think that the age at which people can get Medicare should be slowly raised from 65 to 67. This method is like the one used for Social Security, where the full retirement age has been slowly rising. Supporters say that raising the age of qualifying would lower the number of people who get help and lower the cost of the program. Critics, on the other hand, say that raising the age of eligibility could leave some seniors without cheap health insurance between the ages of 65 and 67, especially if they are not yet qualified for Medicaid or coverage through their jobs.

Increasing Medicare Taxes

Another option is to raise the Medicare payroll tax, which pays for Medicare Part A right now. The Medicare trust fund could get more money to help keep the program going by either raising the payroll tax rate or removing the cap on wages that are due to the tax. Some lawmakers and taxpayers might not like this idea, but it is still a possible way to close Medicare's budget gap.

Shifting to Value-Based Care

Value-based care models are already being used by Medicare. These models reward doctors for providing high-quality care while keeping costs low. Adding more value-based care programs, like Accountable Care Organizations (ACOs) and combined payment models could make it easier to coordinate care, lower the number of times people have to go back to the hospital, and lower total healthcare costs. These changes focus on prevention care, managing chronic diseases, and cutting back on services that aren't needed.

Expanding Coverage for Long-Term Care

Long-term care, like care in a nursing home or help with daily tasks at home, is one of the biggest things that Medicare doesn't cover. Long-term care will become much more important as the population ages. At the moment, Medicare only pays for short-term skilled nursing care and home health services after a hospital stay. It does not cover the kind of personal care that a lot of seniors need, like being locked up. Policymakers have been looking at different ways to increase Medicare's coverage for long-term care. Some of these ideas include making new long-term care insurance plans or making Medicaid's role in helping low-income seniors get long-term care stronger.

Prescription Drug Pricing Reforms

Costs of prescription drugs are a big reason why Medicare spends so much, especially for people who have Medicare Part D. Recent changes, like the Inflation Reduction Act, have made it possible for Medicare to reduce the prices of some expensive drugs and limit the amount of money that recipients have to pay out of pocket. More changes could make it easier for Medicare to discuss drug prices or set price caps on certain drugs, which would lower costs for both program participants and the program itself.

5. **The Role of Medicare Advantage Plans**

Medicare Advantage (Part C) plans are becoming more and more popular among Medicare recipients because they offer extra benefits like dental, eye, hearing, and health programs in addition to regular Medicare. People over 65 with complex healthcare needs may be interested in Medicare Advantage plans because they often have lower out-of-pocket costs and offer more complete care management. As the number of older people continues to rise, more people will likely sign up for Medicare Advantage plans. There are, however, worries about how much these plans will cost the federal government since Medicare Advantage plans usually get more money than regular Medicare. As part of future changes, Medicare Advantage benefits may be made more in line with the real cost of care.

6. **Telehealth and Technological Advances**

During the COVID-19 pandemic, the growth of telehealth services showed how technology can make it easier for people to get care, especially older people who may have trouble moving around or who live in rural places. As the number of older people rises, telehealth and other new technologies will likely become more important in providing care. Medicare already covers more video services, and there is more and more support to make these changes permanent. In the future, changes could include more remote tracking devices, home-based care technologies, and other digital health tools that help adults deal with long-term illnesses and cut down on the need for in-person care. As the U.S. population ages, Medicare sees big problems, such as higher healthcare costs, more people wanting services, and a strain on the trust fund for the program. But Medicare can continue to help millions of older Americans get important medical care with careful planning and focused changes. Looking ahead, **Medicare's future** will likely involve a combination of policy adjustments and technological advancements to meet the evolving needs of an aging population.

Some potential changes include:

- **Raising the Eligibility Age**: Policymakers may consider increasing the age at which individuals can enroll in Medicare as a way to address financial sustainability.
- **Tax Adjustments**: To ensure long-term funding, raising taxes could be another strategy to support Medicare's growing expenses.
- **Expansion of Value-Based Care**: Shifting towards **value-based care models**—which focus on patient outcomes and cost-efficiency—may continue to grow, encouraging better quality of care and reducing unnecessary spending.
- **Long-Term Care Solutions**: Addressing the rising need for **long-term care** services will be a critical aspect of Medicare's future; ensuring older adults receive comprehensive support as they age.
- **Integration of Telehealth and Emerging Technologies**: **Telehealth** and other digital innovations will play a key role in enhancing access to healthcare, particularly for older adults who may face mobility challenges. These technologies can improve care management and streamline communication between patients and providers.

Financial Sustainability of Medicare Programs

Medicare's long-term financial health is a major worry because the program's costs are going up due to changes in the population, rising healthcare costs, and changing healthcare needs. Medicare covers health care costs for more than 65 million Americans, mostly seniors and people with disabilities. It is mostly paid for by payroll taxes, general tax funds, and premiums paid by recipients. However, the program's finances are in danger because the population is getting older quickly, healthcare costs are going up, and there are problems with how the program gets money. **Here is a thorough look at the things that affect Medicare's ability to stay in business, the problems that it will face, and possible ways to protect the program's future.**

1. **The Medicare Trust Funds and Their Current Status**

The money for Medicare comes from two trust funds:

- **The Hospital Insurance (HI) Trust Fund**: This fund is responsible for supporting **Medicare Part A**, which provides **hospital insurance**. Part A covers inpatient hospital stays, care in **skilled nursing facilities, hospice services**, and some **home health care**. The HI Trust Fund is primarily financed through **payroll taxes**, with employees and employers each contributing **1.45%** of wages. Additionally, individuals with higher incomes pay an extra **0.9%** in payroll taxes to support this fund.

- **The Supplementary Medical Insurance (SMI) Trust Fund**: This trust fund finances **Medicare Part B** (which covers doctor visits, outpatient services, preventive care, and medical supplies) and **Medicare Part D** (which covers prescription drug benefits). Unlike the HI Trust Fund, the SMI Trust Fund is primarily funded by **general tax revenue** and **premiums** paid by Medicare beneficiaries. These sources ensure the ongoing operation of Parts B and D, allowing Medicare to cover outpatient care and prescription medications.

Current Status of the Medicare Trust Funds

- **HI Trust Fund:** The Medicare Trustees' 2023 study says that by 2031, the HI Trust Fund will be gone. From now on, Medicare will only be able to cover about 89% of hospital costs unless something is changed. The deficit is because healthcare costs are going up, more people are getting benefits, and the demand for hospital services is not keeping up with the growth in payroll taxes.
- **SMI Trust Fund:** The SMI Trust Fund is backed by general tax income and beneficiary fees, so it is not at risk of running out of money. Parts B and D, on the other hand, are getting more expensive very quickly, which adds to the government debt. As healthcare costs rise, so do the demands on general income, which puts even more pressure on the government budget.

2. **Key Factors Driving Medicare's Financial Challenges**

Aging Population

The U.S. population is getting older quickly. Every day, 10,000 baby boomers turn 65 and can start getting Medicare. Between now and 2030, more than 80 million people will be on Medicare, up from about 65 million today. Medicare's funds are under a lot of stress because of this rise in participation. People use Medicare services for longer periods as they age, especially when they have health problems that need ongoing care. Chronic diseases like diabetes, heart disease, and Alzheimer's disease affect a lot of older people, which makes Medicare costs go up even more.

Rising Healthcare Costs

In the US, healthcare costs are rising faster than the industry as a whole. As a big payer for health care, Medicare is especially at risk when the prices of hospital stays, doctor visits, prescription drugs, and long-term care go up. It's getting more expensive to get medical care because of new technologies, medicines, and more people who have long-term illnesses. Medicare's spending on prescription drugs has also grown very quickly, especially since new specialty drugs with high prices came out. This trend is likely to keep going unless steps are taken to keep drug costs down.

Medicare Payment Structures

Medicare bases most of its services on a fee-for-service system, which can favor the amount of care over its quality or economy. This way of paying for healthcare often leads to services that aren't needed, higher costs, and less efficient care delivery. To fix this problem, Medicare has added value-based care models like Accountable Care Organizations (ACOs) and combined payouts in the last few years. By rewarding providers for better results instead of just offering more services, these models hope to improve care management and quality while lowering costs. However, the switch to value-based care is still in its early stages, and it will need to be widened even more before it has a big effect on Medicare's funds.

Long-Term Care

Medicare does not pay for long-term domestic care, which is usually done in nursing homes or at home. However, it does pay for skilled nursing care and home health services after a hospital stay. The growing number of older people who need long-term care is putting more stress on the healthcare system as a whole. Many Medicare users have to turn to Medicaid or pay for long-term care services that aren't covered by Medicare out of their own pockets.

3.   **Potential Solutions for Improving Medicare's Financial Sustainability**

Medicare is having money problems that need to be fixed by reducing costs, bringing in more money, and changing policies so that the program can continue for future generations. **Here are some possible options that lawmakers are talking about:**

Increase Payroll Taxes

Adding more money to the Medicare payroll tax is one of the easiest ways to keep the HI Trust Fund solvent for longer. The trust fund would get more money if the payroll tax rate was raised from 1.45% to 3% for both companies and workers or if the extra tax on people with high incomes was raised. One more choice is to raise the amount of income that is taxed by Medicare. Unlike Social Security, Medicare does not have a cap on earnings that are subject to taxation. However, more changes could be made to the tax system to raise more money.

Raise the Medicare Eligibility Age

Another possible change is to slowly raise the age of qualifying for Medicare from 65 to 67, so it matches the rising age at which people can retire from Social Security. This would lower the number of people who could get Medicare benefits and make it take longer for people to start using Medicare services. This change would lower Medicare costs, but it could leave some older people without cheap health insurance, especially those who can't get Medicaid or plans through their jobs.

Implement Premium Reforms

At the moment, people who get Medicare pay fees for Parts B and D. About 25% of the costs of these services will be met by the payments. The other 75% will be paid for by general tax revenue. The SMI Trust Fund might not have to spend as much if the rates for Parts B and D were raised for people with higher incomes. One other option is to make Medicare recipients with higher incomes pay more for their coverage while keeping fees low for recipients with low and middle incomes.

Expand Value-Based Care Models

By pushing healthcare workers to provide better, more efficient care, value-based care models like Accountable Care Organizations (ACOs), bundled payments, and Medicare Advantage (Part C) plans could be used more widely. This would help lower costs. Value-based care models try to make things better for patients and cut down on hospital stays, tests, and treatments that aren't needed. The goal of these changes is to change Medicare from a fee-for-service system to one that awards care that is both high-quality and low-cost.

Control Prescription Drug Costs

Controlling the cost of prescription drugs is a key part of making sure that Medicare will be able to pay for itself in the long run. As a result of recent changes made by the Inflation Reduction Act of 2022, Medicare can now discuss prices for some very expensive drugs. However, more may need to be done to allow for more price negotiations, stop price increases, and lower total drug spending. **Among the other possible changes are:**
- Expanding the list of drugs eligible for price negotiations.
- Imposing penalties on drug manufacturers that increase prices faster than inflation.
- Capping out-of-pocket costs for beneficiaries in Medicare Part D.

Encouraging Enrollment in Medicare Advantage

Medicare Advantage (Part C) plans, offered by private insurers, operate under a **value-based care model** aimed at improving healthcare coordination and reducing costs. Unlike traditional Medicare, these plans often provide **additional benefits**, such as **vision, dental**, and **hearing coverage**, as well as fitness programs and prescription drug plans. One of the advantages of **Medicare Advantage** is its focus on managing care more efficiently, helping to minimize unnecessary services and expenses. By promoting greater enrollment in these plans, **Medicare** could potentially reduce overall costs while offering more comprehensive care options. This approach ensures that beneficiaries receive **coordinated healthcare**, which can lead to better health outcomes and cost savings.

4. **The Role of Innovation in Securing Medicare's Future**

Medicare's financial stability will also depend on how well healthcare is delivered, how technology is used, and how payments are made. New technologies like telemedicine, remote tracking, and digital health tools can help lower costs while also making it easier for people to get care and better their health. During the COVID-19 pandemic, telehealth grew a lot. Making some of the temporary changes that were made to telehealth services permanent could help Medicare lower the costs of in-person visits while still making sure that patients get care on time.

Conclusion

Medicare might seem complicated at first, but having a basic understanding can help you make informed decisions about your healthcare. Millions of older adults and people with disabilities rely on **Medicare** for essential services, such as **hospital care, doctor visits**, and **prescription drug coverage**. However, Medicare faces financial challenges due to rising healthcare costs and a growing number of beneficiaries. To make the most of your **Medicare benefits**, it's important to know how the program works, what services are covered, and stay informed about any updates. Whether you opt for **traditional Medicare**, explore **Medicare Advantage** plans, or look for ways to manage your prescription drug expenses, understanding your options can help you access the care you need with fewer hassles and at a reasonable cost.

B

C

N

Q

R

S

T

W

Y